Visions of a Quantum Woman

Barbara,
All love
Jms.

Visions of a Quantum Woman

A Memoir
by
Margaret Rose Duns

Tadorna Press
ITHACA, NEW YORK

First published in the United States of America
in 2018 by Tadorna Press, Ithaca, NY
www.tadornapress.com

ISBN: 978-0-9915781-1-5

Project Manager: Della R. Mancuso
Creative Director: Donna Murphy
Editing: Rick Ball
Cover Image: Brickrena & agsandrew @ Shutterstock

Printed and bound in the United States by G & H Soho

First Printing 2019

1 2 3 4 5 6 7 8 9 10

To my darling Auntie Rose
with a million thanks for a lifetime of love.

Contents

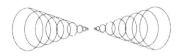

Acknowledgments

I had so much support for writing this book that in many ways I think of it as a team effort. Mack and Carol Travis are major, major influences in my life, and I began writing as a direct result of Mack's insistence. My own dear Meg, who listens to my ideas, opinions, my bleats about life day in and day out and is still there! I am always at your service. Della, who knew I was holding back and teased out the full story, encouraged and guided me through the process and always left a spark of inspiration glowing after her departure. And for giving me the benefit of her first class team, Donna and Rick. Auntie Rose, who knows nothing of this book and probably will not be perturbed by it—she will continue to just care for me. Martha and her husband, Arthur, who made me think outside the box. Jeanie, such a compassionate and generous mentor. Ally and Karen, who kept my feet on the ground with lots of kitchen wisdom and gales of laughter. Charlotte, who has my heart always and whose babyhood brought me to my senses, something she does regularly still. Racheal, remembering all the good things. Julie, for nourishing my brain as well as my body during our cookouts at Mack and Carol's—and for priceless tips on writing. My lifelong family, especially Max and Maureen. How I love you all and know that you love me. My biological family: our journey always seems about to begin. You have my love, support and respect eternally.

I bow down to the Vedic Tradition of Masters enlivened in my awareness by His Holiness Maharishi Mahesh Yogi. They have given me and millions of people the key to our own treasury.

Many of the names used in the book are pseudonyms, including that of the author, Margaret Rose Duns.

The author is British, and glad to be. However, this book was conceived, written and published in her beloved United States; therefore the English used is American English.

There is a three fold structure to the text:
(1) the narrative in plain text.
(2) the visions in italics in their own blocks, and
(3) any commentary on the visions will be in italics immediately beneath the boxed vision.

Introduction

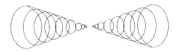

Having lived this life of dross and shared it, helped spread the raw material of it around, I have reached the stage of yearning. I yearn to turn it into gold.

I have been on this earth for more than seventy years and, literally, from day one it has been a time packed with drama and intrigue. Uncertainty has been one of my foundation stones, and far from fearing it I love it, seek it out. I suppose the downside of that is that living a conventional life was not to be my fate.

Born into the British working class means that I never start anything at the top. I start at the bottom and struggle my way to the top, stay there for a while. Like Nijinsky did with his leaps: "I leap and then hang there for a while and then I come down." Then I, too, come down. I repeat this pattern over and over again.

It recently occurred to me that it might make good sense to record in writing some of the more bizarre events in my life, including, as it does, my adoption by a couple called Doll and Frank and some very unsavory experiences in my childhood. If relating my tale has any worth at all it will be in the fact that it may help another person going through similar trials to know that the path has been trod before (by millions) and it is possible to survive and live your own choice of life.

And then there are the visions. If you are unable to relate to the adoption and the brutal childhood, you might be able to relate to the visions.

A beloved aunt once asked me how I had managed to get through all the mud, and I answered honestly that I had "always had something with me." I still call it my "something" and it's still with me, always will be with me. What is it? I do not know.

Throughout childhood it seemed like a very loving friend. I experienced it as existing outside me, and when it visited I felt totally safe and secure, loved beyond any love we can imagine, cared for by something that knew much better than I did what was right for me. Sometimes it was simply the feeling of all those qualities being with me. That would make me very joyful and I would want to dance and sing—even at times when the most dreadful things might be happening.

At other times the experience has been of a second reality coming to exist alongside my everyday reality. In fact, the "extra" reality always seems to be the "actual reality" and the everyday becomes secondary for the duration of the experience. The vision always carries more authenticity, seeming more concrete than the walls around me and the ground I stand on.

These instances have been occurring ever since I can remember, and it took me some decades to come to terms with the fact that they lay outside the usual range of experience and that other people did not have their own "somethings."

I have included my own interpretation of each vision as I relate it to you, even against my better judgment. I was hesitant to do this because I believe it is not possible to communicate a completely accurate understanding of what each or any of the visions is about. Each one seems to have a wholeness of its own and my intellect can only partially grasp at the meaning. So my attempted explanations will reflect only my own level of knowingness, my own ability to fathom something unfathomable. Even if I have managed to secure a very slight recognition of the whole, the visions have empowered me, brought me joy and hope and widened the horizons of my life tremendously.

These days the source of the visions seems to lie more within me—they are more integrated—and it was only when I began to write some of them down that it slowly dawned on me that they are quantum! What a discovery that was. I have lived with a growing familiarity with the quantum level of life ever since I learned to meditate in 1977; and here I was, living it for all these years without understanding it!

I believe my "something" in its many forms has kept me whole when I might have easily disintegrated altogether. But it has achieved something else that I feel may be even more important, although it may not apply in every case. I believe it has changed the outcome of a difficult situation in at least one instance, and that instance is to do with my relationship with my adoptive father, Frank. One moment in a vision changed the future in a way that I could not have foreseen and would never have thought possible. To be able to change outcomes is a mighty, mighty ability and one that I am assuming every individual would welcome.

Although, as I have said, I have had these quantum experiences for as long as I can remember, it has been the regular practice of Transcendental Meditation that has stabilized and integrated them to the degree of them becoming part of my sovereignty over the events of my own life. Just to know that has been an empowering thing for me.

A recognition of quantum physics is becoming increasingly

important to all of us who want to participate in our own future.

In order to make that participation as effective as it can be, it is necessary for the individual human awareness to be able to experience the more subtle levels of life where quantum physics resides and its mechanics are active. Transcendental Meditation is a simple mental technique that facilitates the experience of these levels with ease. Anything that allows us to experience these levels would have the same result—enabling us to utilize the enormous power and energy we find there. I know that I have been able to access this precious field for most of my life, but it was only after learning the technique of meditation known as Transcendental Meditation that I was able to accomplish that at will, rather than having it happen randomly, unexpectedly and without any intellectual understanding of what was going on. Being able to culture the ability to contact the transcendent at will and on a regular basis has made my life infinitely more dynamic, purposeful and enjoyable.

Throughout the book I refer to the concept of quantum physics and provide brief explanations. I hope this will help clarify any wonderings you may have of "what is it?"

Here is my story set out with visions and narrative for you to enjoy. Telling it to you achieves the alchemy I am yearning for.

The symbol used on the cover and throughout the text of this book, the spiral graphic, is known as "The Rik." Vedic Science—the non-religious science of consciousness—acknowledges that all of life as we know it and experience it is, at its source, a wave of sound.

At the quantum level life is singing to itself constantly. When sound begins to transform into matter, it is singing its old, familiar song. On its way to becoming a new sound it makes its way through the first Rik (spiral) and then into the second. "Rrrrrrk" is the sound of creation within the Rik. When the sound emerges, it is singing its own new song. That may be the song that becomes a grain of sand, a bird, a whale, or a human being. Life's song has an infinite range of possibilities, yet the source of all life is the same unified field of pure consciousness where quantum physics has its playground.

CHAPTER 1
Arriving on Time

I am sitting upright in a dining room chair. A man is standing in front of me about three feet distant. He is about to offer me some healing. Before he can begin work, there is a burst of orange and golden light that completely surrounds me, blocking out him and everything else. Someone comes toward me from out of the light. They are behind me. They bend over me and put something in my arms. It is a baby. The being stays for just a few moments as I look at the babe. It is very clear to me. The baby is myself. It is time for me to take myself back into my own possession.

I had gone to stay with my sister, Janet, for a few days in the 1980s. She had some health issues and we were exploring together ways to get her back to health. We had heard of a healer who had a very good reputation and thought it could do no harm to try it. When it came to my own interaction with the healer, the vision I have related above occurred. It interested me afterwards to learn from my sister and the healer that they had both seen the light (both said it was orange and gold and very bright) but did not see what happened inside it. Even though I understood intuitively what it meant, I could not, at that point in time, appreciate the scope of the effect it would have on my life. I will go back to the beginning of this adventure.

My birth, in February 1945, threw my mother into a pit of despair.

She had been married to the love of her life for five months after a whirlwind romance, and only after a week of marriage did she tell her husband that she was carrying another man's child.

The love between them was strong enough to last for more than sixty years, and he responded by saying he would support her and wanted to remain married to her, but he would not bring up the child of another.

They decided I would be put up for adoption at birth.

It was wartime and this was the conservative county of Surrey, south of London.

My mother's husband was serving in the Royal Navy but was given leave to be with her at the time of the birth. The date was set and she was taken to the hospital to be induced at noon. They usually induce labor when they expect complications from a delay, but within an hour and a half of induction I had made my entrance and the wheels of my life were set in motion. The experience of my mother was that I "shot out so fast," as though I "couldn't wait to get on with life."

Janie, my birth mother, and her husband of five months, Chris, were staying temporarily away from their home in Surrey because my appearance and the wedding-date math did not match and tongues would wag. They were in a couple of rooms far from home and hoped the adoption would take immediate effect. But it did not. After some weeks Chris had to return to his ship in Scotland, and Janie was left alone with me.

As she told me fifty years later, she was desperate to be rid of this baby that she hated, and as the days passed she grew more and more despairing. The town we were in was her original hometown in the county of Essex and she had the company of several of her sisters—she was the eldest girl in a family of four girls and four boys. She was estranged from her father and stepmother, and without the presence of her husband she felt lost and alone with a huge burden to bear.

She tried to smother me, but her nerve failed her.

Then one of her sisters told her of a mutual friend of theirs, Dolly, aka Doll, who was grieving deeply for the loss of her own baby daughter to crib death.

Was this the way out?

On May 8, 1945, Victory in Europe Day, Janie and one of her sisters, Lucy, carried me to Doll's home. They had to make their way through the tables and chairs being set up for the street party that afternoon, one of the thousands of such parties held all over the UK that day.

Doll was, apparently, in no state to make a coherent decision. She had been unable to work since April 1, when her daughter had died, and had suffered a complete nervous collapse.

However, Doll's bedridden mother was clearheaded and able to set terms for the deal. Janie was to have no more contact with me—ever. I would be brought up as Doll's daughter. My Aunt Lucy told me many years later that when everything had been agreed, Doll grabbed hold of me and held me fast.

Janie and Lucy left, and it was to be forty-seven years before I saw my mother again.

A few weeks later Janie's youngest sister, Rose, aged fourteen, came to see me in my new home. She was to become one of the most significant figures in my life—a loving presence and support in spite of all my ups and downs. Back then in 1945 I was lying in my buggy, she said, in the front garden and she peeped around the hood to see me. Her heart leapt at the sight of me and she knew she could never leave me. She asked Doll if she could keep in touch and Doll said certainly she could. Such a simple request from an impromptu visit and a ready assent from my new mother was to provide me with something stable to hold on to when life's storms threatened to extinguish me. Seventy years later Rose is still a most loving influence in my life. I was a bridesmaid at her wedding; she and her new husband came to see me just after their wedding and took me out for days of fun; every birthday there has been a card from her; and her door is ever open to me. She is my darling Auntie Rose, and dedicating this book to her is such a small thing to do in return for a lifetime's love.

CHAPTER 2

Early Days with My New Family

> *I am three years old and wearing a flowery dress. I'm sitting in a little cart with wheels in the dark gray backyard of the house of one of my new aunts in the East End of London. There is nobody else around. I feel something inside me slip—something nice is going away, something that had always kept me warm and safe. Now I feel the gray cold. I see an ethereal, cloudlike form and almost sense, rather than see, the womanly face and outstretched hands floating slowly away from me. I feel panic. I've never been without it. I have to stay here, I know, but it must stay with me. As it rises in the air against the backdrop of the gray-black brick of the yard wall, I feel isolation filling my space. No! No! No! I don't want to be here without you. I stretch out both my arms and plead for it to stay.*

The memory of this incident sank into my unconscious. All my life I have had a clear recall of playing alone in my aunt's backyard and the feeling of peace that pervaded me in that grim, cramped space. I always felt happy there, and the memory would come now and again throughout my teenage years and into adulthood.

I don't recall exactly when this vision came back to me—it was more a case of reliving it than merely remembering—but when it *did I recognized it with thrills throughout my physiology. The feeling of the cloudlike form was as fresh as the day it first occurred, even though I did not understand any significance it may have had. Its remembrance brought me great joy and comfort, as do all memories of the visions. Even when the "message" of a vision may be something fearful, I have never felt anything but bliss and joy associated with the visions. It is as though fear cannot abide with the visions— it is robbed of its negative power somehow. Here only, when I am three years old, I feel panic and a sense of loss that I find difficult to explain. It may well be that I knew more then than I know now and knew I did not want to live without some wonderful presence that I had always had with me and that seemed about to leave. Or perhaps a three-year-old feels fear more keenly than an older child.*

Even now, I cannot say if the "intelligence" in the cloud remained with me or left that day.

The first year of my life had been eventful. Separated from Janie, my birth mother, I lived in Essex with my new mother, Doll, and her parents in a three-bedroom house on a quiet street. Doll's mother was an invalid confined to life on a chaise longue in the downstairs living room, and she passed away shortly before my first birthday. Doll always spoke very highly of both her parents. Her mother, Nell, had been strong and independent before she became ill. As a member of the Women's Social and Political Union—which later became known as the Suffragette Movement—she had traveled to Wales to join miners and their families in their protests about wages and working conditions. Once she had her two children she had taken them most places with her, to community events such as tea dances, "whist drives," rummage sales, etc. As a result, Doll and her brother, Brian, had learned ballroom dancing while still very young and could glide across the floor effortlessly as though on skates. Dancing together was a real joy for both of them.

But then Nell began to lose her energy, and the creeping sickness that was to kill her gradually immobilized her. Doll took the purse strings for the household and much of the responsibility for day-to-day life. She left school at the age of fourteen and took a full-time job as a machinist in the local factory. Brian enlisted in the armed forces and left home.

Doll's life is a little foggy around this time. I know that she married young and stayed living with her parents. She once told me that she decided she didn't like being married—it had been just more work for her to do.

Then, in 1939, the war came. Her husband was conscripted and went abroad. Doll continued to run the household. Her father worked in London during the day and was out most nights.

Doll became pregnant in 1944 after a brief affair with an itinerant serviceman. Her marriage over, she gave birth to her daughter, Linda, just after the stroke of midnight on December 31, 1944.

Doll hardly ever spoke to anyone about her daughter, but she and I talked about what happened on a few occasions. She told me that on April 1, 1945, she had picked Linda up out of her crib to feed her before going out to work for the day. Linda's head fell back and Doll knew instantly. She ran out into the street with Linda in her arms and didn't stop running until she got to the local police station. There she was told that Linda was dead. Crib death.

At that point, Doll's narrative would end. Nobody was told about the effect this had on Doll, and it wasn't until I began probing into the circumstances around my arrival in her life that I started to appreciate how devastated she had been. Devastated and vulnerable. She seems to have had a mental breakdown, sitting at home with her mother, staring at the floor without any interest in life.

Doll's silence, almost secrecy, about parts of her own life applied also to the whole of mine. Somewhere along the line the decision was made that I should not be told—ever—my own story, which began with Doll on May 8, 1945.

On that day, a month after Linda's funeral, Janie and her sister Lucy had turned up at Doll's door with me. After they had left, Doll and her father had prepared a bed for me in a drawer— Doll would not put me in a dead baby's bed, she told me.

So our life together began. Many years later Doll would say to me, just once, "You straightened me out." She said it almost reluctantly and with a bitter edge.

Not long after Doll's mother's death, Doll's father remarried and left the house. Her brother, Brian, moved back in after an accident ended his army career, and he brought with him Ruby, whom he soon married. The four of us—Doll, me, Ruby and Brian—lived in the same house together, and then Ruby introduced Doll to her brother, Frank. So that made five.

Doll's father had signed the house over to Brian, being the male in the family, assuming he would be fair and responsible about Doll's needs. He wasn't. One evening when Doll came home from work, Brian told her she had better pack her things because he had sold the house and the moving van was coming in the morning to take us all to the East End of London to live in the same street as Ruby and Frank's family.

We moved into a house that had a green door divided into two vertical halves, so that you could open one half and enter without opening the other. I loved that door.

Ruby and Frank's parents lived on the other side of the street with the children who were still at home, which was most of their brood of thirteen. Dave, their youngest and Frank's brother, was eight months younger than me, and by this time Ruby and Brian had a son, Marcus, who was two years younger than me. Dave and Marcus and I were inseparable for the two years we all lived in the same street. We three adore one another still.

There were so many young people in that small street—most of them ours—that when we moved around the neighborhood together it was more like a swarm than a group of people. I remember Frank's family as noisy, rowdy, always hungry, with their winter underwear sewn on. In those days it was not uncommon for old-fashioned mothers to sew a child's woolen undershirt to their "long johns" to ensure all-round warmth and comfort for the entire winter. Laundering was not the main priority in those days! The clamor could get disturbing sometimes. But most of all I remember loving them and being loved by them lifelong without question.

Time rolled by, there in the East End. Doll, Frank and I shared one room and it was pretty cramped, but my memory of it is of a happy time. It was not the same for Doll and Frank, however. There were many family-wide arguments, and pieces of Doll's jewelry that went missing, with her own brother the prime suspect. Ruby even reported Doll to the authorities as an unfit mother.

Doll was considered a single mum by the local authorities,

and the climate for single women with babies was culturally hostile for both mother and child, so Frank's presence gave some protection. However, when Doll explained the circumstances of my arrival in her life to the bureaucracy, all obstacles fell. Because of this I was allowed to start full-time school at the age of four, instead of five. It fitted well with the working day.

Doll had to be made of strong stuff to withstand the trauma of having no home of her own but living in the house of her brother, whom she could not trust, and a sister-in-law who was happy to keep an eye on me while Doll went to work but wanted to exact payment in the form of taking over Doll's role as mother to me.

The day Doll took me to my first day at school, we nearly marched to the redbrick building; her hand was very firmly holding mine and we went straight to the head teacher's office. The head was such a nice lady and she took me along to the huge classroom where I immediately bonded with a little girl called Barbara. I felt very happy at school and loved learning to read.

School was to mark a major difference between me and my new, adored family. Frank's family line did not value education and considered it something to be got through as quickly as possible. I, however, was to take the path of education seriously, albeit with a few time lags between grammar school and university, leaving school at age fifteen—which was then the earliest possible age—but returning to university under my own steam at the age of thirty-two to get a degree. I am a lifelong learner.

At about the time I started school, Doll, Frank and I went on a glorious trip!

It was my first ever trip to an amusement park. The colored

lights were all on. It was dusk and we approached a stall—me holding tightly on to Doll's hand. There were legs and noise all around me. I wasn't as high as the stall but I could hear the owner greeting everyone and inviting them to do something.

Frank stepped up. I had no idea what was going on but I loved looking at the lights on the stall.

Then there was a shout. Frank had done something good and the man in the stall was asking him to choose his prize.

There was a row of fluffy toys, all pinks and blues.

Frank scratched his chin, not knowing which one to choose.

My eye fell on a bear with pink and blue fur and the most beautiful brown button eyes. He was mine and I was his forever.

I was not a child to ask for things. So I wished and wished hard. I have never in my life wished so hard for anything. I wanted that bear with all my four-year-old heart.

Frank chose a lamb. I stood rigid. "No, not that one, Frank," said Doll. "It's got too many corners—she won't be able to cuddle it. What about that koala bear over there." The very bear I had set my heart on.

And he was mine. The man on the stall handed him to Frank and Frank gave him straight to me—I can remember the huge watermelon smile on Frank's face.

I took that bear to bed with me every night. He had a fascinating fragrance—wood shavings. He was, in fact, a burlap bag filled with wood shavings and would not pass today's strict criteria for child-safe toys.

I loved every speck of his sawdust. I would cuddle him so hard he would start to crunch and I'd inhale his fragrance and feel comforted. Anything that had not been perfect in my day would dissolve once I shared it with Teddy.

11

Teddy became my repository of love. He still has that evening at the amusement park, the lights, the wish, my mum's hand and my dad's smile woven into his being, just like me.

I recall a friend of mine telling me about a trek she made in Asia. She said that on one of the pilgrimage trails there had been a hut. The invitation to pilgrims was to leave in the hut, forever, your most treasured possession—as a sign of growing self-reliance.

When she went inside she found the hut full of teddy bears. My memory of life with my family begins with finding Teddy.

Everything I have written up to the point of the amusement park was related to me by Doll, and much later, Janie added details pertaining to her part.

When I began to form my version of events based on my own perception, life became much more complex, confusing and at times dangerous.

Doll was technically a single woman, and single women were not legally allowed to adopt children. She had to live with the knowledge that Janie could claim me back at any time. Adoption therefore had to take place as soon as possible.

Doll and Frank married in 1949, and I remember helping them move our few possessions on a handcart to our new home in Stepney in the heart of London's East End, sometime after that. From then on I would see Frank's extended family only during infrequent visits.

Our apartment was on the top floor of an apartment block that had been condemned by the local council, so we could expect to be rehoused someday.

We had to carry everything up eight flights of stairs, and

the result was us standing in a room with a panoramic view of the locality with its trolleybus wires and busy street life. It was just heavenly!

Doll and Frank were free at last.

From time to time we would go to Essex to visit Nannie and Grandad Duns. He was Janie's father and Nannie was her stepmother. That made him my biological grandfather. Janie's own mother had died suddenly at the age of forty-one, leaving eight children aged from thirteen to two years old to be cared for by their father, who had to work long hours to keep the family financially afloat. In those days, if a lone parent was unable to care for their children, the children would be placed in a children's home—perhaps together, perhaps not. Grandad wanted to avoid separation at all costs, so within a few months of becoming a widower he married a widow with three children of her own. It was to be a platonic relationship, at Nannie's insistence—a marriage of convenience for the sake of the children. Janie, my mother, had been twelve at the time of their wedding and had been told nothing of the arrangement until she came home from school one afternoon to find Nannie in residence with her children.

Their house was large, with chickens in the yard, and when I was around, Grandad was always laughing. I wasn't yet as high as the kitchen table, and on one visit Nannie invited me to go into the walk-in pantry with her to choose what to have for tea.

It was beautiful in the pantry, full of jars and cans and fresh eggs and milk. I was looking around when I felt Nannie's arms around me. I looked up at her. Her face was red, and tears were streaming down her cheeks. She hugged and hugged me, all the time trying to be quiet so those outside would not hear.

I said nothing about it until I was well into adulthood, but the memory has been with me always, clear and sharp.

Their home seemed very welcoming to me and my parents, and I was to see them regularly throughout my childhood. Grandad used to come to visit us now and again in London, and I remember his jolly presence.

I had no idea of their relationship to me until I was fifteen years old.

Grandad Duns became very active in the adoption process. He hired a King's Counsel whom I remember as Uncle Stan and who came to see us on a couple of occasions.

On May 24, 1951—Empire Day—at the age of six, so I have been told, I had to go to court with Doll and Frank to appeal for special leave to adopt. They won the day and I was legally theirs from then on.

On that day Janie gave birth to her third daughter, Marie.

CHAPTER 3
Life Gets Serious

By the time a year had passed and I was seven years old, my life seemed very different.

Doll seemed to change. I couldn't seem to please her no matter how hard I tried. She was always angry. Frank was always angry. There was a lot of shouting and throwing things. I seemed to be always "in the way."

One by one, my favorite toys would disappear. When I asked about them I would be told that they were in the "dolls' hospital" and I would get them back when they were better. But they didn't come back. I continued to wait and hope until the day I came along the landing from the bedroom to the street door to see my mother, Doll, taking out the trash in a bucket. There, sticking out from underneath all the screwed-up paper and floor sweepings, was the pink fluffy ear of Teddy.

I screamed and started to cry, begging her not to throw him away.

She was very angry with me, but she grabbed the ear, pulled Teddy out and threw him at me.

I stopped asking after my lost toys.

Something from those days stands out in my memory and will not go away:

Doll and I were at home alone. I had run from her into the sunlit, multi-windowed living room that hung over the busy main road. I was feeling pent up and miserable and wanted to be by myself to recover from her latest storm. She followed me into the room, eyebrows arched in anger and snapping like a terrier. My resistance arrived as I yelled "Mummy, Mummy! Stop! Stop!" and I reached out to push her against the wall, my fingers clamped around her elbows. I was crying and laughing at the same time, afraid of the strength of my own emotions.

She could have pushed me away and freed herself easily—I was less than half her size. But she stood where I had pushed her and, without moving her head, looked down her nose at me, looking up at her, and said, cool and slow, "You are a murderess. It is written all over you. One day you will murder someone."

How to cause permanent damage to a young life. It was so cold-blooded that it frightened me for many years—made me afraid of myself. And I still shiver when I think of it.

Now I realize that this was the period when she was hoping to get pregnant again. There were one or two miscarriages at this time.

Lukewarm to cold, push to pull to push. That was how my relationship with Doll was developing. Incidents like the early school attendance tell me that she must have loved me to hold on to me when her position was so vulnerable, but that vulnerability may have been what made her hold on. I loved her with all my heart from childhood to today and spent a lot of time trying to work out what I was doing wrong. I was to learn in the years ahead that Doll was a complex personality who preferred the people around her to stand on shifting sand, while she seemed rock solid. It was about power.

> *I love going to bed every night. I climb between the cool sheets and know that I will soon be in a beautiful place. Sleep comes almost immediately and I am somewhere full of color and bright light and surrounded by people who are very happy to see me. They are very tiny people and we frolic and laugh and they show me their world. It's always the same there—beautiful and fun—and I can't wait to tell Mum about it in the morning. She says it's fairyland.*

Going to sleep has been one of my lifelong loves. Left to myself I would sleep ten hours every night and during my teenage years would often sleep a straight twenty-four hours over a weekend. It's never been the case that I feel sleepy during the day and take a nap. Throughout the day I am active and alert. It is the actual process of climbing into bed, turning out the light and knowing that nothing will disturb me until the next day. It brings me great joy and it happens every day! If I encounter any strange and wonderful lands during sleep these days I am completely oblivious of it. Deep, untroubled sleep continues to be a great blessing to me.

Speaking of fairies…

I remember Doll taking me to see the Disney movie *Peter Pan* when it first came out. At the part where Peter asks everyone who believes in fairies to clap and so save Tinker Bell's fading light of life, I smacked my hands together until they were sore and my arms ached. Even as a politically aware adult, I still believed in fairies, but one doesn't talk about these things generally because responses can get very heated. A powerful subject!

Over the years the children in our family, especially, would buy me pictures and figures of fairies as birthday/Christmas gifts, and Doll bought me a wall hanging about fairies when I was in my fifties, giving me a knowing look as she said, "This is very important to me." I thought it was nice and kept it close by me.

Then, out of the blue, came the information from Doll that I used to see fairies as a small child and would tell her and Frank about them.

What! When? When? Give me an example.

"Oh, we would be in a café and you would tell me there was one on the sugar bowl. I would ask you what it looked like and how it was dressed, and you would say, 'It's just like us, only very, very tiny.'"

She said I stopped reporting the fairies at about age three.

Then the penny dropped.

So this was why I had shelves of fairies, cards and pictures all over the place! They all knew, didn't they! The whole of my immediate family knew and I didn't. More than that, it had been a closely guarded secret. Another one. Another secret about my own existence that was everything to do with everyone else's life and nothing to do with mine!

However, this news was uplifting and I quietly absorbed it and got on with my days. It sharpened my observation, though, and there were times when I felt the family thought I was a fairy. It fitted, of course: someone from somewhere else— another dimension, another planet, even. An alien. "No wonder she's not like us."

On occasion I would say something during a conversation that must have come from a place outside the boundaries of the family's thought processes and there would be a silence, sidelong glances, and the subject would be changed. I have to say, though, that these instances did not feel at all oppressive. It felt rather more like me making my mark and gave me a somewhat brief respite from the overarching atmosphere of "eccentricity" that came to be an often-used term to describe me.

Sixty-three years after my last reported sighting of fairies, I saw something that I have chosen to call a fairy. I was lying under a tree beside a much-loved lake and looking up through the canopy with the light streaming through. It was blissful. Then I saw a perfectly round circle of light moving through the branches about three feet above me. It moved slowly, backward and forward, up and down, and then it turned and I saw a tiny figure inside the light. I doubted my own eyes and thought it had to be an illusion. Then the light moved across a branch and dropped behind it, its top half in sight and the bottom out of sight. So, I thought, it can't be a reflection because the light has not refracted. It has literally gone behind the bough of the tree.

After what seemed like a long, long time I "came back": my senses adjusted back to "pre-fairy" mode. The light had gone. But the experience is still there in my being, soft and light and wondrous.

I was in a very expanded state of consciousness, as though the whole world were at my command, but I would not describe this experience as the same thing as one of my visions. The fairy did not seem to belong to another level of reality that came to join mine—rather, it is always right there where it was on that day, and whether or not I perceive it depends entirely on my ability to tap into that level of everyday reality. The experience did not seem to occur in order to address a particular event in my life. It felt like a tap on the shoulder from something familiar—something that belonged to me and I to it. Another hello. Something had not forgotten. Something remembered me and came to tell me it is still there. That was the feeling.

Early in 1953, Doll and Frank got successfully pregnant and I was given the news in a very sweet way—I was going to have a little brother or sister and it would be wonderful. I was so excited.

Together we planned what kind of crib, stroller, coverlet the baby would have.

Doll continued to work until she was six months gone. That was the way it was done in those days. She was absolutely huge and ate three pounds of oranges a day.

It was August and school was out, so I had a glorious time at home with Doll for a few weeks until she went into hospital for the birth.

It was to be a caesarean section and would involve a longer-than-usual stay, with plenty of time before and after the birth to monitor how things were going.

Frank and I went with her to the hospital and I was assured that I would be able to sit with her.

The British hospital rules at that time were lethal for kids. The senior nurse on every ward was called the ward sister.

Among other things, she was there to make sure the rules were strictly enforced. There were women's wards and men's wards and children's wards, and the rules said that no children were allowed on the adult wards. Visiting times were between 6 p.m. and 8 p.m. each day, and children, healthy or unhealthy, were definitely not welcome.

What happened next is one of the many reasons why I believe the British culture, at bottom, does not approve of children.

When we got to the ward, Frank and I were told to wait outside the glass doors and Mum disappeared inside. I was able to see her go behind a screen, and when she emerged she was in a nightgown and climbed into bed.

This was not what I thought was going to happen. I thought she would go in, be given the baby and come out again. I pushed the door to go to her.

The ward sister told me I was not to go in.

I screamed and cried and fought to get to the door, but between them, the sister and Frank held me down.

I was told I would not see my mother again until she came home.

She was in the hospital for three weeks.

I'm still furious about it.

Those three weeks changed everything for me, and I kept quiet about it for fifty-five years.

I was now at home alone with Frank.

CHAPTER 4

The End of Childhood

Frank and I did not have a good relationship. He and I knew one another for sixty-two-plus years and never had a conversation in all that time. He was an inarticulate man of very little formal education, and any attempt to talk to him always led to him getting furious, shouting with eyes bulging and bringing his huge hand down on some part of my body.

I was not going to enjoy the time without my mother. To say I was frightened doesn't cover it.

Imagine my surprise...I was in bed crying my heart out that first night without Doll when Frank called me over to get in bed with him and be comforted.

Yes. It happened. What is known in some traditional circles as "a secret sorrow with the father" and in today's sharp world as sexual abuse. I'm still furious. I hated him with a cold, dismissive hatred for the next thirty-two years.

Every time I was alone with him I felt in danger, and sometimes I couldn't get away and had to endure it.

I was twelve when menses began. Of course, my parents had told me nothing about it, but schoolyard speculations had given me some pretty wacky ideas of what to expect. Every month was torture. The pain in my abdomen would be like a fire that cramped and torqued my innards until I lost consciousness.

If I was at home, Frank would have to "rescue" me from wherever I happened to be—the bathroom usually—and carry me to my bed. My worried mother would leave him to it. As I regained consciousness I would be aware that his hands were inside my clothes and running all over my body, massaging my pealike breasts as they went.

It was not even safe to be unconscious.

Oh! Little girl. Little girl. Whatever tides ran through you at this time were translated into feeling. You had no words, no voice, no way of understanding anything of these events. You needed guidance, joy and love, and what you got was a parent's madness that knocked the stuffing out of you.

As the adult you, I have a voice. I want to be your spokesperson. I have to travel back:

She is eight. She stands alone in a dark space. She is becoming aware of a stirring of energy inside. She is used to living in a storm of feeling that tosses her ship around constantly. This is different. It draws her attention. It is peaceful, coherent and stronger than the storm. Sounds seem to come through the atmosphere to her. The sounds take the storm and transmute it.

Everything is vibrating in sound—her body, the air around her, the stars and planets, the universe. The words are coming closer and she feels strong, strong enough to take everything that is headed her way. It is sudden—the collapse of the words from the macrocosm to the microcosm—and she is all at once the repository of this new energy that is clarity, surety, eloquence.

She has something to say and realizes that she is no longer alone. People are around her in her wilderness. They, too, are drawn to her unuttered words. Millions of people, from embattled places. There are Afghanis, Palestinians, Iranians, Iraqis, Africans, Latin Americans, Native Americans. The impoverished. They speak as one child's voice: "Stop it! Stop it! How dare you invade my environment without my permission!" The feelings run high and electricity runs through every hair, every muscle, every eye. Dust rises. The earth shakes. They are shaking, shaking the earth. And then they are gone.

She stands alone, no longer in a wilderness, and the words come loud and clear: "How dare you touch me in that cruel, crude way!" "How dare you make my life such a bitter, torturous struggle!" "How dare you insult my mother by doing such a terrible thing!" "How dare you make me frightened out of my wits every minute, every hour of every day!" "How dare you usurp the role of the one to awaken my sexual nature!"

She is shaking her fists, stamping her feet, and the words run in torrents, telling her tormentor what she thinks of him, spitting at him until she delights in her own anger and the clouds inside her dissipate. She begins to feel some relief. She is empowered.

If only that vision had occurred then, when I was eight years old, but it didn't. It happened recently while I was thinking about the day's writing. There have been other experiences where the two of us have been consciously together in the vision, but in those the child has been informing the adult. This is the first time the adult has been informing the child. However, it feels like a huge breakthrough for both the adult me and the child me. It was as though the past has been changed by the present. To be there, with myself as I was all those years ago, and not only "with" in the sense of being present but also in the sense of actually being myself at age eight, brings me such a powerful feeling of belonging. It wipes away memories of alienation, then and now. It makes me feel more whole and gives my life a level of authenticity, as though the fact of my existence has some real significance—is very important—to something, somewhere.

As I write I feel the exhaustion of those years. My constant vigilance was not enough, but growing older helped a lot. The torture ended by the time I reached my teen years, but unfortunately he was still alive.

I remember now that on my fourteenth birthday Frank and his brother Les went out for a drink—they were not habitual drinkers, having been brought up in a home with a drunken, violent father. Frank came home reeling with rum and had to be put to bed. As Doll and Les got him into bed he kept repeating "I'm sorry, Marg," "I'm sorry, Marg." He must have said it more than a dozen times. Doll asked me what he was apologizing for, and I answered honestly that I didn't know. I can still hear the sound of his apology, like a mantra, coming down the hallway to me standing at the end wondering what was going on. The fact is, in order to have any kind of life at all, there were long periods when I submerged the debilitating memories and tried to lead a "normal" life. This must have been one of those times. Some sense of preservation propelled me toward a future that was not ruled by my father's acts. Time was drawing me in to a sense of my own life and what I wanted it to be. I must have blocked out the misery at that time, and it was well into adulthood that I recalled his apology and what it was about.

How and why the horror stopped? I would have to step into his madness to answer that.

Perhaps it was my being older and more of a presence, not just a passive recipient of whatever my parents chose to bestow on me. I did sometimes think he might have changed over the years. The one and only other time he tried it on, I was fifty-seven years old and he was a semi-invalid. I was stronger than him this time and fought him off. But the old, old feelings were revived and my night had been spent trying to make some sense of the constant stream of horrific thoughts going through my head. The next morning I was so wrought up about it after a sleepless night, I told him never to touch me again—ever. He said "Sorry, sorry" rapidly.

Telling him that had a cathartic effect. The fear left. The fury remains.

Back to 1953 and the first remembered experience of abuse. I don't know how many days I had to live like this, but a soon-to-be aunt came to see us, took one look at me and took me home with her to her parents' house in Kings Cross.

I had a wonderful time there. They baked me pigeon pie,

gave me ice cream and made a fuss of me. After a little while I came out in hives so badly I could not walk. My legs were like tree trunks. The doctor said it must be an allergy—probably to ice cream.

I wish I could give you a beautiful vision to take all this junk away, but the beauty that was a constant in my life did not always take the form of a vision. Sometimes it was like a blanket of love that came and wrapped itself around me. It carried a very clear message: it loved me unconditionally, and it brought me great happiness even in the most difficult times, so that I would feel a surge of joy rush through me and would want to dance and sing. It was tangible and ethereal at the same time. And I didn't think anything of it because I was a child and didn't know that it was unusual. I just enjoyed it.

I always felt bigger than Frank, even as a very young child. Perhaps this was my protection.

On September 2, 1953, my sister, Janet, was born. Ten days later she and my mother came home. By that time I was back at school, and on the glorious homecoming day I raced home. I yelled up to the window from the street, "Is she home?" Frank nodded. I flew up the eight flights of stairs, through the street door, heart pounding. She was in the kitchen sitting at the table. I launched myself at Doll. There was no response. She sat like stone and turned her head away. The shock went through my body as wave after wave of shudder. I broke into pieces and put my whole energy into patching myself up in order to live. "Don't you want to see your sister?" she said, nodding at the crib at the foot of the table. I walked up to the crib and saw a pink mottled body lying there.

That's how it was from then on. Now that Doll had her own daughter again, my usefulness had expired. It was to take me decades to allow that particular truth to take its place in my psyche.

My experiences with Frank during Doll's absence had delivered an almost mortal wound to my being. The thought of having my mother back cannot be underestimated in its promise of safety and security. To have that shattered so immediately, so definitely, left me bereft for the rest of my life. It was a moment of uncompromising, evil truth and I wish I could have been spared it.

I realize now that Doll and Frank had achieved their own dream. They had a child of their own. I was like a tool that had served its purpose and was no longer relevant. In spite of the many evidences of this being the case, I refused to see it that way and must have made a decision to carry on regardless. I do not recall having made a conscious decision to become a tightrope walker, but that is effectively what happened. I kept my head down and tried never to do anything that antagonized my mother. I needed my mother and would not let go of her under any circumstances. I welcomed my baby sister and loved helping to care for her. I dreamed of our companionship in the years to come. Somehow I managed to evade bitterness and jealousy. But I lived a millimeter above the line of despair. It was to be a long time until 1992, when the tightrope walker met her Niagara.

CHAPTER 5

Don't Tell. Don't Tell

I am an adult woman and it is evening. I am in a place that is very beautiful. Large flowering shrubs line my path. The stars are out and I am ambling slowly on the path beside a slow-running river. I come to a widening of the path and see to my right a small, arched wooden bridge.

In the middle of the wooden bridge a little girl is standing. She is wearing a blue-green coat and hat and looks about three years old. She sees me and is overjoyed. Her arms are thrown up in greeting and she waits for me to reach her, jumping in anticipation.

I am filled with joy and love to see her, and I reach down to lift her up. As she leaves the ground in my arms I become aware that she has come to uplift me. She is me when I was three years old. All is well with her and cannot be anything else. She is joy. She is bliss. She is relaxation. She is wisdom. She is high in my arms and we rub faces and smile at one another. The love we feel for one another is too subtle, too fine, too deep to easily put into words. I have found her. She has come to me. We will never be parted again.

I will always be so grateful for this vision. The feeling of strength from the three-year-old me—strength and joy—is with me always. She came so gently and she changed my life forever. She gave me such a certainty of always being with me, of "How can we ever be apart when I am you and you are me?" My life is supported by her. It's very simple and totally mind-blowing. I sometimes dare to believe that every person has this simplicity and joy, this connection, until they are three years old. Then it becomes submerged by the complex and challenging experiences of being in the world.

Is this what I felt myself losing in the cart in my aunt's backyard that day? I wonder.

I was eight years old and already had a lifetime's drama packed into my existence. There was to be no slowdown for me as the years passed.

At this point, in 1953, I was just living it all as it came, just like all other children, and had no idea that what had happened to me was unusual. My environment became more and more eccentric as I watched the adults around me communicate in extraordinary ways, ways that seemed to indicate that there was something amiss and it had to do with me. There was a lot of whispering and nods and winks in my direction, so much so that I came to expect it whenever I was around adults. The feeling that there was something different about me grew stronger, and I became so astute at observation and seeing and separating what was hidden from what was revealed—so quick to pick up nuance and contradiction—that I became a kind of emotional detective without even knowing what that meant.

One thing was certain to me: what was hidden behind the nods and winks was much more important than what was said openly.

I had to bide my time as a child and take it all in my stride. If I were to ask what it was all about, it could blow something sky high—and that something might be me! Better to let it all go on around me and get to know the atmosphere of it, learn to live in it without rocking the boat. It made life seem very precarious, while it systematically turned me into an object. Any right of reply, right to question, to participate in my own life was denied. Everything about me belonged to them. The only thing of my own that I had was my intellect—and that intellect was honed and sharpened over years of silence and the habit of always referring things back to myself. I learned to analyze my environment—the reactions of the people around me to me and to one another—in order to make sense of the chaos of intrigue and half-truth that lay on the surface.

I went deeper and deeper into myself, peeling away layers of understanding in order to fathom the depths of truth.

I am standing in the school playground with noise and flying kids all around me. The steps up to the school entrance are about three feet away, and the wall is giving me a little shelter.

It is warm weather and this is one of the first days back after the long summer break, so it would be the first week of September. This will be my last year at John Scurr Primary

School. I am therefore ten years old.

I am a little pillar of total silence in that melee of activity. There is something coming into my mind—I can't quite catch it. I have to stay perfectly still and listen.

An impulse comes to speak the words out loud. I speak them out as they are forming—no idea what they are until I hear them: "I have a brother, and his name is Tony." It means nothing to me. Life continues.

Janie, my birth mother, had given birth to her fourth child, a son, on August 24 that year, so he was about two weeks old when this playground incident happened. His name is Tony. I met him in January 1992.

This experience came when I was on the brink of learning "accidentally" that I was not the child I thought I was. My parentage, the one thing we always take completely for granted, was about to yield its huge question mark and switch my life to another track.

There was something there, lying in hiding, waiting for me to discover it. Even then, I realized that what was waiting for me was me, and it was thrilling. It was exactly the opposite of life as it seemed on the surface. The deeper I went into my own being, the more open, honest, loving and secure my life seemed to be.

I longed to tell my mother about what had happened while she was in hospital. Why do children keep these things secret? I cannot answer that. The reasons are archetypal, primordial and many. Being a victim often makes one assume blame. I remember not wanting to upset my mother. Fear of reprisal was very real.

The man was around me most days, of course. I would avoid eye contact, make an excuse to leave the room if we were alone, emotionally cling to my mother, but I never said a word. The term "fear" does not cover its effect on me then—and for the rest of my life. It changed me in a most destructive way. I became extremely watchful for any sign from him that he might be heading in my direction.

I was living in a minefield, but the earth in the field was teaching me about its richness, the abundance of wildflowers we would see in spring, its own nourishing qualities. My attention would always rest on those things, those hidden things of my own, and over time my father lost his place in my life. He was the mine that could destroy me if I put a foot wrong, so I had to watch my step at all costs, but there were other, much more beautiful things that drew and held my attention.

I have to say that if some event had occurred that had taken him away from my life forever, I would have been very happy about that. Death would have been the best. But his staying power was strong. He withstood my undisguised negation of his existence for thirty-two years, until something changed, and we fought a desperate, toiling battle against one another every day of those years.

And my mother never noticed.

Have you ever come across a person who seems to know what is going on with everyone else but has no idea what is happening under their very nose? That was Doll.

Counselors and psychologists have told me it is pretty certain that my mother knew what had happened between Frank and me. It was too awful, of course, and as on other occasions with other awful truths, Doll closed her eyes to it and lived within her own fabricated world where everything was good. Anything that threatened her with the truth was rejected with a shocking display of venom, as I was to discover much later.

I am an adult woman and am walking toward something in a huge, pure-white room, full of air and sunlight. As I approach the far wall of the room I see that there is a maze of massive white blocks—as big as tea chests—between me and the wall. They were invisible until I came very close to them. There is a jagged path through the blocks, and I carefully tread the path. It leads first to the right and then to the left. Then I see her.

She is standing against the wall, fragile but resigned. She is a thin, dark figure. Her hair is plastered flat to her head, and dark, oily tendrils hang over her forehead and ears. Her eyes are dark—dark circles underneath them as though she has had no rest for a long, long time. She gazes straight ahead but seems to see nothing. Her mouth is a grim, straight line.

She looks so ancient, but I know she is eleven years old.

This vision told me that by the time I reached eleven years of age the inner me was almost catatonic. I had done very well at school but was about to move on to a different establishment of education, a grammar school for girls that lay in an unfamiliar part of the city. Grammar schools, before they were abolished, were actually single gender high schools for the more intellectually 'advanced' students from age 11 to 18 years. So I was on the threshold of change, but I know that it was not the prospect of change that created my almost dissolution; it was what I was having to cope with at home.

The Quantum world is not bound by time as is the classical. Even though I was well past eleven years of age when I had this vision, I knew that it was as significant for the well-being of my inner and outer self as it had been at that stage. Anything could happen.

The year I was eleven stands out in my memory for several reasons. It was the year I left my beloved primary school and began to attend that grammar school for girls in the City of London, and it was the year that Kitty came.

Kitty was a woman the same age as Doll who had lived with my aunt and uncle, Ruby and Brian, for some years. She was severely disabled with osteoarthritis but was able to work full time as a machinist in a factory that made ladies' coats.

Kitty was feeling exploited by Ruby and Brian and wanted to move out, but her family lived in Suffolk, hours away, and she wanted to stay in London. What was she to do? She spoke to Doll about her desperation, and negotiations began as to whether Kitty should come to live with us for a while. These negotiations involved nobody but Doll and Ruby—arch rivals in the family. Frank and Brian were completely excluded, and so was I.

I was standing near the elevator that brought people from ground level to the fourth floor, where our apartment was. We were now living in a much less interesting apartment block in another part of the East End.

The elevator door opened and out stepped Kitty. Her eyes were blazing and she spoke to me in staccato fashion: "Is yer muvva at 'ome?" "Yes," I said, and she stalked off in the direction of our door.

Do I want that woman to come and live with us? No, I do not. She's crabby.

I began to think about the implications of Kitty coming to stay.

In the last months I had found myself being consulted by Doll over the dinner table about various details of the day, and we would sometimes sit in conversation for a while before clearing the dishes. I was purring about this. I was Doll's friend, and I loved it.

If Kitty came, I could see that Kitty would become Doll's house friend and I would be relegated to the ranks. I decided I wanted Doll to ask me how I felt about Kitty coming.

Doll never asked me.

Kitty came "for two weeks until she found somewhere else." She stayed for forty-seven years!

And I was right. She became Doll's friend and I sank back into oblivion.

Much as I came to love Kitty over the years—she was a sweet, demure soul between bouts of anger—I never, ever forgave her for taking my mother away from me. She died in 2002 and I still don't forgive her. Once she was there I didn't stand a chance with my mother, and my loss felt so very heavy.

The months rolled by and I felt like a piece of wallpaper in the house. For all my mother seemed to care, I just did not exist.

There was no asking me how I was, what was going on at school, who my friends were, how my lessons were going, had I cleaned my teeth and washed my hair. It was back to the usual cycle of neglect.

Something must have really rankled with me, because I remember deciding that I was going to make her notice me by hook or by crook. I was not going to wash my body or my hair or clean my teeth until she noticed. That was it! That would work! She'd soon realize I was missing her...

Two months went by. I stuck to my heroic regime and my friends at school kept their distance. Then "Nitty Norah, flea explorer" came to the school. In other words, the nurse employed by the school system to check on our general state of care and cleanliness.

I remember being in the line with the other girls waiting to be inspected and peeking under my socks to look at the seams of grime on my feet. It came my turn to be seen and I mentally checked out while Nitty Norah went through her routine.

Nothing was said to me. Nothing at all. And I am so grateful to that nurse for her lack of rebuke.

However, the next thing I knew, I was being marched by Doll to the dentist, where practically every tooth in my head was filled—and many of those black fillings are still in my head today.

I was so lucky I did not lose all my teeth!

Doll said nothing to me. But my point was made. I felt able to join the human race again and began using soap and water.

Did Doll give me more attention as a result of this? I just do not know, but I remember feeling satisfaction at having done something that left her in no doubt about my feelings toward my life.

She was never going to be an attentive mother. Photographs of me at that time show a child dressed in shabby shoes and a grubby coat with most buttons missing.

CHAPTER 6
Truth Comes Looking for Me

When I was twelve I found a document among my mother's things that proved that my father was not my father.

There was no sense of relief, of wonder. I just thought, "Who, then, is he, and what is he doing in our lives?"

I had been with my mother before he came along. He was the intruder, not I.

There were documents—divorce papers, and an "In Memoriam" card for a baby girl buried in April 1945 at three months of age.

So, I had been a twin!

Even though I could see that the months of our births did not match, I clung to the twin idea for a long time. It was pretty neat.

Then one of the nodders and winkers told me that I was, in fact, adopted.

Wait a minute! This meant that my mother was not my mother.

That can't be true. I didn't want that to be true.

Even though I had liked and respected the person who told me, I made sure never to see him again.

Never give a child bad news about themselves.

I remember riding home on the bus immediately after being told, but I don't remember what went through my head.

I kept silent for three years, and then one evening my

mother said, "You know you're adopted, don't you?"

My mother was really the Wicked Witch of the West. She brought me up during one of her stopovers in the East End of London. I loved and adored her and will continue to love and adore her until my last breath, in spite of the fact that she rolled me out flat time and again and tried to stuff what was left of me out of sight.

So now I knew that Auntie Rose was my "real" aunt and I knew that Nan and Grandad Duns were my "real" grandparents.

These were tremendous gains to make to my life in one evening, but my losses were heavy too. Other grandparents, aunts and uncles, cousins, all of whom I loved and who loved me, were no longer mine. We have loved one another continuously ever since, but I have never quite recovered from the loss of them on that night.

My mother gave me my "new" family details as I sat on her bed that night. I listened without questioning. I knew by then that it was a tinderbox and, although ostensibly all about me, was in fact just as much about the whispering adults and I had better leave well enough alone. My observations over the years led me to believe that I alone should be in charge of my life, but I was still young enough to be controlled by these adults. I was going to have to wait quite a while before picking up my own reins. I decided to accept what the whispers told me and just get on with life.

I have the eleven-year-old girl by the hand. She is listless and silent and I am worried. We are walking through some undergrowth. At some point I see that the jungle we are in is very lush and we are following a path. I see animals and insects. They are all golden.

After a while we come to a clearing. There is a one-story house in the clearing. Very neat, clean and orderly. Someone comes to meet us. It seems we were expected. The person is bronze skinned with very dark, thick hair. A clear, open face with a welcoming smile. They seem androgynous. S/he seems very young—perhaps in early teens—but we all know s/he is eternal. Eternally young. We stand together for a moment and I feel at a loss. I feel her hand still in mine. I want to know the name of the golden person. Wordlessly, I am told it is Marion. Marion knows the turbulence I am experiencing. S/he does not address it. The feeling is of loving compassion and lightheartedness. I take the girl's hand and put it in Marion's. Marion nods reassuringly, as if to say, "She will be fine; I have her now."

I turn to walk away, and Marion and the girl walk into the house. I set out back through the jungle with a heavy heart. A few moments later I hear a joyful giggle and then gentle laughter, and the cloud lifts from my heart. I walk back through the jungle, seeing golden animals from the path. I know this place well, but now is not the time for me to stay...

Years passed between the first vision of the eleven-year-old as a child in catatonic shock and the one related immediately above. But they were classical years, years in which I lived and moved in the world as an adult. The Quantum reality is not tied to time—past, present and future coexist at that level of life in a continuum. I was able to witness and participate in the rescue of the young inner me through this vision. No matter that it happened years later, the Quantum me was able to take me, as her, to a healing place where she would be made whole again and the damage of the past would be repaired. And that would affect the present and the future in one stroke.

I will always be breathless with wonder about what this vision achieved.

My life as a human being in the world staggered from crisis to crisis. I married the first of my three husbands at age twenty-one and expected to settle into a pretty good life.

What a daydream that was!

The wedding itself was a dream of a day. It poured with rain but there was such happiness, and the reception went off so well with a live band that had everyone up and dancing and playing silly games that made us all laugh. It went down in the family annals as a real event to remember.

I had enjoyed a wonderful courtship with Robbie. He was the youngest of five children and had nieces and nephews just a few years younger than me. Life with them was full of laughter, and I shared the limelight with Robbie as the center of the family.

His family had all been in the heart of London throughout

the Blitz and told many stories of life in wartime London. When the air-raid warning siren howled they would drop everything and run to the nearest Underground station, a few hundred yards from their home. They would have blankets and bedding down there from the night before and would settle down to try to get some sleep, but with people elbow to elbow it must have been difficult. There was music and singing and soldiers on leave with their girlfriends, and "You had to close your eyes," they said. Those were special days, and sweethearts never knew if they would see one another again.

To listen to them you would have thought life on the subway platform the most delightful of experiences!

Then there was the day when they came up to find their home had been destroyed by the bombing. Robbie was less than a year old. They lived for a while like vagabonds, going to the ruins of their home during the day and searching for water and a means to cook food. Then they had been offered an apartment in a sturdy housing development built by a trust—a legal body set up by a philanthropist in the nineteenth century who wanted to improve the living conditions of working people. The apartment block was just around the corner from their old home and it had seemed like heaven. They lived there ever after, and as the children grew up and married they took vacant apartments on the same estate. It was like a quadrant of family nestled into the clutch of squares—Tavistock Square, Russell Square, Woburn Square—in London's West End. All the families knew one another in that quadrant, and the mutual histories were tattooed on every brain. The generations grew up together; they played football together in the quad; the girls went dancing together, hoping to meet a prince, and by and by they all settled and began the whole rigmarole again.

From the very start, I felt blessed to meet Robbie's witty, warm family and loved just sitting and listening to their many stories, which always had a hilarious punch line. Those people still keep me warm at night.

Then Robbie and I had that beautiful wedding and rode off into the sunset together.

The curtain came down and there we were, on an empty stage. We didn't know what to do with one another! It was time to grow up.

I found myself with two full-time jobs—one in the City of London and one running the home, cleaning, shopping, entertaining. I was mostly alone; my husband would come home late at night without explanation and resisted any kind of participation in home life.

We had many friends, and most weekends were spent with them, but if there is something wrong between husband and wife no amount of friends can fill the gap.

Childhood abuse is cruel in so many ways. One cannot list them all, but one important effect—of abuse and also of adoption—can be that if a time comes when all is not right in your personal life you jump to the conclusion that it is your fault, because you have been damaged by the experience of abuse and/ or adoption. And that may be true. There is damage—layers and layers of damage—but it may not be responsible for everything that is not good in the life that follows. There was great passion between Robbie and me, and we had enjoyed a level of loving intimacy during our courtship that was based on a deep sense of wanting to be together, to enjoy one another.

Then we got married and everything changed dramatically.

I am looking back at myself now. The surroundings are familiar. I am in my London office in Drury Lane, Covent Garden. I am secretary to a man who is chairman of ten companies. I have worked for him for almost seven years. I am twenty-seven years old.

The way I march into his office shows me that I am very, very annoyed. I am carrying a thick file and I walk up to his desk and slam the file onto it. This anger is uncharacteristic of me at work. I am always happy there. I get on well with everybody in the company. I can do the work with my eyes shut.

This vision puzzles me still. What stands out is the fact that I am twenty-seven years old and not some other number in the twenties. Is twenty-seven a significant age? I wonder. Is it archetypal? Or is it that I began to seriously question the validity of my marriage at about that time? It is true that the thought of being without a husband and doing something else with my life began to germinate then. My job was enjoyable and I felt I spent each day with friends, but I was still doing someone else's bidding, just as I was doing at home. Perhaps this vision catches me at the point where I am becoming restless and dissatisfied with the way my life was going.

I had ahead of me changes in my role at work, and I was to discover that, while I was treated with great respect as long as I remained in a servile role, once I crossed the great divide into management it was a very different story. The glass ceiling was so real to me I can still feel the bruises from bumping against it time and again.

However, years later, during my second marriage, I was to find great fulfillment in running my own small business for nine years and, on the basis of that experience, becoming a management trainer at a prestigious UK business school. My creativity was allowed to blossom, and I employed original methods using theater and my own design of teaching activities to enable my entrepreneurial students to learn through their own experience in my lecture room. I loved the work and was very successful at a time when it was difficult for anyone to make a living in the university environment (the business school was a postgraduate school affiliated to a major British university).

I certainly had found what I was good at, but I was absolutely no good at the corridor politics. I was directing the first British postgraduate training unit for women in business, and when it became perceived as a threat to the established male order in the training world, it was rubbed out.

Any thoughts of career were far distant, though, during my marriage to Robbie, which amounted to nine years of slavery. His wonderful family espoused the concept that at home the man is master and the woman does everything for him. Robbie gleefully took his stand behind his three older sisters, who had fetched and carried for him throughout his life. Can you believe it—I thought he would not be that way once we were married! How naïve was I!

While he was out playing rugby, cricket, soccer, etc. I was at home cleaning, cooking, running errands. Nine years of that plus a full-time job, and I was emotionally and physically exhausted and saw nothing ahead in my life except a huge brick wall.

That turned out to be a very good experience, that brick wall.

When Robbie was publicly disturbed while having sex with a young unmarried woman at a New Year's Eve party we attended in December 1975, I reacted calmly and compassionately. Two weeks later, on January 13, I left a note on the mantelshelf saying goodbye forever and walked away from loneliness, insecurity, his wonderful family, my steady job in London, and stepped into the unknown with ten pounds in my pocket.

I made one telephone call—to Doll at her place of work. I told her that I was leaving Robbie and coming to London on my way elsewhere, that I couldn't tell her where just yet, but that I would be in touch very soon. She begged me to call in at her office when I got to London. I did. I was surprised when she pushed some money into my hands and asked me to meet her and Frank that evening. I suggested a pub not far from their home, one that Robbie did not know. I knew he would pursue me if he could.

We had an hour together at the pub, and Doll was frantic for me to stay close to her and Frank, saying she would call a friend and ask if I could stay awhile. I couldn't do that. "If you know where I am, Mum, Robbie will pull every fingernail out until you tell him."

If he caught up with me before I had some time and space to myself I knew I would regret it for the rest of my life. Doll wanted me to go home with them for an hour, just to consider. No way!

When Doll went to the restroom I apologized to Frank for bringing this to their doorstep, and he told me he didn't care about it at all!

They took me to Liverpool Street station. Doll said she must know where I was going but I said I could not tell her yet. I would tell her as soon as I got there—I would be all right and she should try not to worry. We both got out of the car and I hugged her goodbye and told her I loved her. Then I turned away and walked toward the station. I don't know what made me look back, but I did, and Doll was standing, wringing her hands, with tears literally streaming down her red blotched face. I had to force myself not to run back to her and tell her I would stay with them for just this one night. But something made me turn around again and continue walking into the station, my heart like a stone.

Robbie was sitting in their living room when they got back home.

I booked into the YWCA for the night and looked up where I could get a return train ticket to for ten pounds. I figured I had to be able to get back to London, where I could easily get a job, if things didn't work out.

Bristol it was. The next morning I was on an early train out of Paddington bound for Bristol Temple Meads. It was January 14, 1976.

I settled into a four-seat cubicle with a table, feeling like a bird let out of a cage. I sat with my back to the engine, looking at the London skyline receding and the rolling hills of the country landscape coming into view. I felt a sudden stab of panic. What if things didn't work out as I hoped? What if I didn't like it, didn't make it, couldn't earn a living? I looked away from the window and into the railway carriage.

There, sitting next to me and in the two seats on the other side of the table, were three shining beings. Their white light was so bright I could not see detailed features, but I could see how very happy they were and could even see their reflections in the window. They were nudging one another and their shoulders were shaking with laughter. My fear dissolved. It was going to be just fine. Just fine. And it was.

This vision was so glorious! It took me from doubt to determination in one stroke. I was a changed person as a result of it. From then on I knew I was going to be all right and, more important, that I had done the right thing in extricating myself from such an abusive relationship. I was to discover things that would make me strong for the future—that I was not alone in this, that many women suffered these hardships within marriage. These were still days when leaving a husband or wife carried social penalties, and this vision swept my apprehension away forever.

I had six of the most wonderful years of my life ahead of me. Years that would take me to college, bring me into contact with friends I still cherish today, and enable me to explore my creativity in ways that I feel few people have the opportunity to do.

Doll was just wonderful. She wrote me often, especially in the early days, and kept my whereabouts secret from Robbie, who pestered for information. I still have a dish towel that she sent me with a picture of a girl sitting on a suitcase and the words over her head "I just know things are gonna get better!" What could her support mean other than that she did love me! I felt I had won my mother back, and that felt so, so good. The thought of being able to spend time with her again made my days sunny. I would even be nice to Frank if it meant reconciliation with Doll.

Robbie turned up at my place of work in Bristol on a Friday night six weeks later. He had used unlawful means to find me. He pointed out how much weight he had lost. I was lodging at the YWCA, so we walked all over Bristol in the pouring rain over that weekend. He began with begging and, when that didn't work, turned to threats. At one point I opened my mouth to say "All right. All right. I will come back." I couldn't stand the torture. But the words would not come. They just would not come and the moment passed. On the Sunday afternoon I walked with him to the bus that would take him to Temple Meads station and back to London. His last barb was that if I allowed him to leave on that bus he would never want to see me again. I breathed a sigh of relief and couldn't wait for the bus to depart. I didn't know it at the time, but his next wife was already waiting in the wings. When he returned home without me she took up her position in his life, and they were to have three children together before parting acrimoniously.

It was on Bristol's Blackboy Hill a year later that I saw a poster in a bookshop that really turned my life around. It marked the end of being bullied and scared for the rest of my life. I was in the habit of sitting up all night talking politics with friends from all parts of Europe. We could recite and define exactly what was wrong with society, with the world, but I was becoming increasingly bothered by the fact that we obviously didn't have a clue how to put it right. Feminism provided me with my template for an ideal life, but it was going to take a long, long time. Becoming friends with women who had been through similar experiences made me aware of the great strengths we shared as women. My feminism went through a phase of "man-hating" but I came to consider that a waste of my time and energy. For forty years now I have focused my attention on the amazing beauty of women: strong and brave and resilient. What a fabulous resource we are in our world

The poster I saw that day bore a picture of Maharishi Mahesh Yogi holding a bunch of flowers and advertised a free lecture on Transcendental Meditation.

I learned the technique. It took an hour and a half on each of four days. You are taught the technique one-on-one at the first session, and the other three sessions go into how to use the technique correctly and give you an intellectual understanding of any experiences you may have during those early days. I felt utterly transformed from the first moment. I had more energy, my mood swings disappeared as I became more content and just simply happy. It was all so easy. Without realizing what I had done, I had taken up the path of peacefulness.

Life seemed to continue pretty much as before—all was

smooth and enjoyable—yet when I look back on it now I can see that the effect of meditating was like being on an ocean liner at full speed ahead and suddenly turning 90 degrees in the water. Everything was shaken up and rearranged, but the experience was of gentleness, an easing of pressure and more relaxation in life. I felt absolutely wonderful. From the first meditation on that first day of instruction, I knew that I would do this technique for the rest of my life.

When I think of what has happened to me since learning to meditate I am in awe of the wealth of experience I have had that I could never have thought possible for someone like me. But that experience has been a strong mixture of welcome and unwelcome. I have been challenged to the point of disintegration, mainly because of my own drive for freedom. It's likely, I feel, that the meditation gave me the strength to invite those challenges. In other words, I have to include in my thinking that my beloved meditation really made everything hit the fan! So, do I regret learning to meditate, to transcend? Certainly not! I now know who I am on several levels, I have seen my responses in very difficult situations, and my life is now the sort of life I like to live. I feel free. Freedom, I have heard it said, never comes easily. This is true in my case, but it is worth it. It is definitely worth it. It has been, and continues to be, a story of expansion without end. Huge blocks to progress and obstacles to growth have been smashed along the way, and my life stands now on the threshold of an ever-open door—one that leads to all the things I could wish for.

But wait a minute. This is my life we are talking about, the life that brings challenge after challenge, is full of ups and downs and hard work, of constantly starting at the bottom and working my way up to the top only to go crashing down again to the bottom and starting again. Yes, that's right, that's my life. It's still that way. The difference is that I enjoy every minute and hardly ever feel fear or uncertainty anymore. I think that's pretty good.

Having said all that, it is also true to say that my whole life seems to be threatened by impending disaster.

Things were going to get much, much worse later on, but in the meantime I got my degree, went on a sailing trip from Lancaster in England to Spain, and came very close to death at sea. In April 1983 I married again. Marko was, and still is, a sweet, gentle person and we were very happy for a long time. Until my baggage caught up with us in 1992.

Having never set foot on a sailing vessel before, here I was, a crew member on a forty-seven-foot Scottish lugger heading through the Bay of Biscay. My watch was from twelve midnight to four a.m. each night. I had spent the first half hour sitting on deck in the blackness, feeling, hearing and seeing the moonstruck water. It was obvious that it was working itself up into some kind of frenzy and that in a couple of hours I would be sitting in a tiny shed inside a boiling kettle. And so it was.

At two a.m. I stationed myself on the bridge and kept an eye on the compass. Goodness knows why: we had a very new automatic pilot system and a beautifully made engine to augment the sails when necessary. The sails were down and we were using the purring engine.

The wind started to howl and the boat started to toss around. I kept my eye on the compass. Having something to concentrate on helps avoid seasickness. I had been there for over an hour when I looked out at the sea, which was by now throwing waves up at eye level. There in the water I saw my sister, swimming as though at a beautiful resort on a warm summer's day. She had a bright yellow bathing cap on that had nylon "curls" all over it. Very cute. Behind her came her nine-year-old and three-year-old daughters. The three of them were laughing and having such a wonderful time of it, moving through the ten-foot waves with ease and grace. Then I saw my mother and my Aunt Kitty, swimming a little way off from my sister and nieces. They were more serious, but certainly not troubled. They were all calling out to one another and waving to me, when onto the scene came Frank. He never could swim, so he was on one of those pedal boats for two people. He had on his best overcoat and his never-to-be-forgotten flat cap. He was having the time of his life. Shouting to the others that they were "daft" to swim when they could stay dry on the pedal boat. I stood and watched them all for quite a few minutes. It seemed completely natural and not out of place at all. I don't remember feeling any surprise.

Then, quite suddenly, they were gone—all except Dad. He was still there but without the pedal boat. Now he was standing in the water looking at me with a huge watermelon smile on his face. As I looked at him he stuck both his thumbs up, nodded and laughed. He was resisting for as long as possible the calls from the others that it was time to leave. Then he, too, was gone.

I remember feeling completely matter-of-fact about it and returning my attention to the compass. At that moment, I saw the needle quiver sharply and I watched it stagger around the compass for a moment or two. It was four a.m. and the captain was on the bridge to take over the watch. I told him what had happened to the compass a moment before he arrived, and he began to run checks. Then we woke the rest of the crew. Life jackets on all round.

The cable that operated the steering mechanism from the rudder had snapped and we were now wallowing helplessly in a force 7 gale. The crew was galvanized into action.

Precious minutes had been lost checking the system, and the opportunity to check our position had evaded us. The boat had been swinging violently and there was no knowing which way she was facing. The cable had to be repaired but we had no replacement parts. If we did nothing it was pretty certain that we would lose the boat to the storm.

While people rushed to and fro I came to terms with my lack of experience and realized I had no idea what to do next.

I sat down in the cabin and tried to pull the disheveled strands of myself into some kind of order. The captain rushed by me and, for an instant, our eyes met and I could tell he wanted to give me some words of comfort but couldn't. That was when I realized how bad the situation really was.

I remember feeling an icy coldness creeping up my body from my feet. It felt like the approach of death. Then I became calm.

There was nothing I could do except stay in the background. And hope. A thousand things must have been going through my head, but I simply cannot recall what they were. I remember, instead, feeling almost settled inside. The wind was by now roaring and I could see the black waves reaching up higher than the cabin. It was cosy in the cabin by comparison. The crew had done what they could. They had decided to use a wire coat hanger as a temporary cable, but it had to go around the outside of the rudder and be connected to the steering mechanism just inside the stern.

Who was going to volunteer to dangle over the side of the boat and thread the wire through the rudder? Marko came forward without a moment's hesitation. A slight, quite shy chap who seemed not to fit easily into social situations. He was destined to become my second husband. Marko took the by now straight piece of wire—so frail looking—and went out onto a deck that was shuttling back and forth like one of those "cakewalk" rides at amusement parks. I waited on my perch inside the cabin for a few minutes. But I just could not do nothing.

I went out on deck and saw Marko's feet crossed around one of the deck rails at the stern of the boat. The rest of him was over the outside of the boat, reaching down to the rudder with the wire, trying to thread it over the rudder and through the stern to the two crew who were in the aft cabin waiting to grab the wire and connect it to the steering. I looked over the side of the boat.

It seemed as though the exposed rudder was dangling over a pit of blackness twenty feet deep, only to plunge down that twenty feet and go underwater every so many seconds. And all the time the upward waves were equalling the pit—rising twenty feet above us all around the boat in a crazy game of tag. I lay flat on the deck and grabbed Marko's ankles, thinking that at least I could hold on to him if something went amiss. I don't know how long we were like that, but at some point Marko started to haul himself up from the stern and pull himself back on deck. We made our way along the rocking and rolling deck back to the cabin. The crew had successfully connected the wire and we were back in business. However, we went over the lifeboat drill and decided who would go and who would stay with the boat if she became unsafe.

We were by no means out of the woods yet. The boat had some direction and pull now, but we were still caught in the gale.

An hour or so later, the dear old sun came up and the gale slowly left us for richer pickings. We had three days of drifting around the Bay of Biscay, not knowing where we were headed, when a passing oil tanker gave us the opportunity to radio and get our position. Then we were back on the right course. And alive. There was no jubilation aboard. Just relief. Another three days of blue skies and calm seas and we arrived in Portugal.

A crowd gathered on the harbor to watch us come in—almost as though they knew we had had trouble.

A fisherman gave us his catch of sardines as we moored. The lifesaving coat hanger snapped just as we tied her up. I've often thought about Marko's and my actions that night. He was an unmentioned hero. What I did was helpful to nobody but me.

I would rather have died participating in what was going on than cowering in the cabin waiting for disaster to strike. I only hope that, for Marko, having a pair of human hands trying to hold him fast brought some comfort. A sailing friend later told me that one freak wave would have taken us both overboard. Even though Marko indicated that's the nature of sailing and you just have to deal with things as you go, we all knew it was a pretty close call. Inside I had felt calm and peaceful. Because my dad had told me that everything was going to be all right.

It is very true that my relationship with Frank (dad) was always hostile. Why, then, do I change my mood by saying that I felt calm and peaceful because he had told me that everything was going to be all right? This is a very subtle point and I continue to marvel at it, not only through my own experience but as a result of observing and hearing about stories of abuse from others.

Every child longs to be able to respect their parents. Love is the natural emotion for a child—to feel anything other than love for a parent seems unnatural and even a strain. All through the years of pain, fear, anger there had always been a deep longing for it all to change. For something to wipe away the misery and leave us as a happy family at long last.

To see Frank reluctant to leave me that night at sea and to know he wanted me to be safe, appealed to that child's wish for a good father. Even though I was adult when it happened, to have even a brief glimpse of how I would like it to be – how I wished it could be—made something inside relax. I was able to let go— even momentarily—of the constant vigilance and allow in to my awareness the possibility of being part of a happy family.

So you see that what makes a parent's abuse so dastardly

is the fact that the child longs to be able to love and any true sign of genuine love allows hope to rush in and swell the heart. When all the negatives come back, as they generally do, we are once again bereft. The child always wants to be free to love his/ her parents and to be denied that most basic of desires is most, most cruel.

This was a close shave! It should have been the most frightening experience of my life, and have no doubt I was very scared. During the crisis I had no recollection of the vision of my family in the sea that evening. Just a few hours later and yet it was gone. I attribute the fact that I was able to compose myself and do something, even if futile, with a clear, calm mind while the storm and the danger were at their height directly to the comfort brought to me by the vision and its prophecy that all would be well. The "thumbs-up" from nature.

I don't know when I first remembered the vision exactly, but it could have been when I got back to London and my family a few months later. I was a little surprised at their response: no derisive laughter or disbelief with comments about my eccentricity. They were touched to their core and delighted to know they had been of some help—even though they knew nothing about it at the time. We bought a cake to celebrate.

CHAPTER 7
A Moment of Grace

It is 1985. I am living in the Northwest of England with my second husband, Marko, and together we are running a natural foods business. I am forty years old. I have just finished my morning meditation and I sit up, ready to stand up and get on with the day. I see Frank, in the room. He is standing still and looking at me. He is wearing his gray herringbone overcoat. He seems both very close to me and at the same time very far away. It is dark all around him and I am in my bedroom hundreds of miles away from Frank, with the sun streaming through the window. I am also in the vision, standing facing my father but a good distance from him. (The quantum nature of the visions means that they take place beyond time and space. Therefore, people and things may seem near and afar both at the same time. This is not at all confusing to the one having the vision, but is a challenging concept to relate using the written word.) We look at one another in silence. Then I hold out both arms to him and say, "Come on, Dad, let's forget it." Then Dad disappears.

A sequel to this vision came when, two weeks later, I stand outside my parents' home in London. I ring the doorbell and

> *Dad opens the door. As we look at one another he breaks out into a huge grin and his face looks radiant. I see a dark cloud lift from his shoulders.*

This vision still astounds me. That I should address Frank in that way was nowhere on my agenda. I had intermittently taken professional counseling about the childhood abuse over many years, and it had all been about learning how to cope with it and its aftermath. Never had there been any suggestion of such an approach, and I would not have tolerated such a suggestion! The inner me and the inner Frank, however, were not bound by our human attitudes. Something else had to happen, and the quantum reality stepped in and made sure it did happen. The trauma and years of anger held rule over us and nothing was going to change that. But I know that my quantum "something" was privy to greater knowledge than either Frank or I, and it took the lead in spite of us.

The effects of this vision are ongoing, and I may never be able to work out intellectually the process begun here. I trust my "something" more than I trust myself. It will work itself out in its own "time."

Until that time at the door, I had never realized that Dad, who had a winning smile, had never used it when he saw me.

From that day and for the next twenty years Dad and I underwent a radical change in our relationship.

And yet, nothing changed on the surface. Nothing at all.

I was still very wary of him and he still maintained silence around me. I was still furious with him and treated him with cold disdain. But everything had changed. Everything. At the same time all was still exactly the same. We had no conversation.

He even made a grab for me in later years and I fought him off. I knew I always had to be on my guard and could never relax in his presence. So what, exactly, had happened?

I don't know what happened, but a love began to grow between us. Slowly and determinedly over twenty years we learned to love one another in a silent, undemanding undercurrent of everyday life. Nobody noticed. Neither of us said anything about it. It happened in spite of us. It shattered everything about us, while maintaining the attitudes, behaviors and assumptions we had developed over our lifetimes. It left us intact while it blew everything into tiny pieces and sent those pieces to the far reaches of the universe.

Something had gone forever.

The only word I have for what happened is forgiveness. I certainly had not forgiven. Dad had not forgiven. But something had forgiven. Something had forgiven him and me. No matter how hard either of us may have tried to bring things back to the normal we knew, no matter how much we invested in hating one another, that love continued to grow, unacknowledged but known to him and to me. What had been unforgivable on the human level had been forgiven on the quantum.

The clouds in my heart no longer dominated. The memory of what had happened between us was just as strong as before, but it was now deprived of energy. It lost its control over my moods, my expectations and my self-confidence.

Now, after forty years' practice of Transcendental Meditation, I have been able to reach an understanding of this experience that satisfies me on all levels—emotional, intellectual, experiential, scientific. This is the first of my visions that led me to quantum physics in order to find an explanation for something that defied my logic in everyday life.

The world now accepts that what scientists have been positing and exploring for the last hundred years or so is true. We have a new paradigm for reality. What we experience as everyday life is like the tip of the iceberg. Newtonian physics, where the cosmos is experienced as a huge machine, takes us only so far into universal existence. Quantum physics takes us much deeper into life, to a field where there is intelligence and liveliness and knowledge and where human consciousness plays a pivotal role. Where we have the possibility to become the creator of our own experience. In other words, where we are able to tap into the ability to not only see our lives from many angles at one and the same time, but we are also able to perceive the past, the present and the future simultaneously. And, most importantly, decisions we make at that level are carried out in our everyday lives.

This means that quantum physics enables us to change our own future—if we are operating from a level of consciousness that aligns us with the field of quantum mechanics, itself the nuts and bolts of Mother Nature's switchboard.

The first question one would ask is: "Am I able to change my future in any way I want?" The short answer to that is yes— and no! You are able to change it in any way you desire, but the fact is that in order to get to that place in consciousness in the first place you are required to align your own individual consciousness with the greater cosmic consciousness that runs the universe, so that anything you desire will automatically be in alignment with what is best for the existence of everything in our universe. That is nature's brilliant insurance against human limitations: there can be no mistakes made on that level of life.

It is a level of supreme intelligence, supreme efficiency, supreme power. Human intelligence comes nowhere near it. This level of life faultlessly runs the whole universe without even a glitch and has done so for eons. What a lot we stand to gain from forming an alliance with it, when we are unable to run this single planet without threatening to destroy it at any moment!

Transcendental Meditation gives us access to the whole field of subtlety underlying our everyday life. It is a completely natural thing for us to do—to make contact with it regularly, to form a living connection with it. This simple practice—so simple a child of three can enjoy doing it—leads us to the quantum level of life because that is where we naturally belong. We just forgot about it during the long passage of time.

To bring this back to my vision of holding my arms out to my father and saying "Let's forget it":

I believe my visions come from the quantum level of life. They are a phenomenon of consciousness. When my consciousness is in an altered state I am able to perceive things that cross the boundaries of time and space.

That day, in my bedroom, there was the vision of my father and then I became active in it. I invited both of us to "forget it." Without knowing intellectually what I had done, I had changed the future for both of us. I had dropped a desire into the quantum level of life from that level itself. During the visions I become quantum myself, which means that all things become possible for me. When a person is quantum any desire that comes up at that time will be quantum also, which means that the desire and its fulfillment become the same—no time lapse between the two. By desiring that we both "forget it" while I was quantum the thing to be forgotten had simply been wiped away, eradicated.

From my everyday perspective I couldn't care less about Frank; my feelings did not change. But from the quantum level of life I must have wanted to end the conflict because peace is naturally preferable to war. Perhaps he wanted that also. I may not have been the only actor.

When I speak of an "altered" state of consciousness, I am speaking of a state brought about in a gentle, effortless, natural manner through Transcendental Meditation. You should not try this at home with any tablet, pill, drink, powder or any other "artificial" or "instant" means of changing your awareness. I think there is plenty of evidence to show that this can literally "blow your mind" because you cannot break down the doors to consciousness without paying a high price through your physiology and even your sanity. The simple truth is that your physiology has to be cultured through a gradual process in order to experience these alterations, so that when it happens it is not only awe inspiring but also safe. When it comes to opening that huge, huge door it is much easier to use the key than a battering ram.

Something came to mind as I wrote that: "Knock and the door shall open. Seek and ye shall find."

First, we have to knock. Meditation is us tap, tapping at the door of eternity, and if our practice allows us to transcend our own thoughts, joyful entry is guaranteed.

Something else to consider is why the experience of trans-cendence—of taking the mind beyond the source of thought—should play a part in an experience of this sort. I have thought about this a lot over the years and feel that it is a question of like dealing with like. When something so traumatic, so anti-nature as sexual abuse occurs, the wound goes very deep into the psyche, much deeper than we know. In order to transform that experience and heal the psyche, reparative action has to take place on the same level as the damage itself. When we go beyond our own source of thought we easily reach that subtle level of our own being and are able to put right even the most awful sufferings.

In November 2007 Dad lay dying in my sister's home. She and I had done all we could to make him comfortable and he was surrounded by loving family members. On the Tuesday morning I was alone with him in the house while others did the shopping and made quick visits home. The local doctor was coming to give him a brief examination.

The doctor arrived, a huge, unfriendly man wearing the most gigantic black shoes I had ever seen. I remember wanting him to remove those shoes before they defiled the room where Dad was lying, but I said nothing. There was a diffuser in the room sending out a fragrance designed to allay anxiety.

Dad was lying flat on a single bed. He had not communicated much for the last twenty-four hours but was able to respond with "Yes" or "No." The doctor asked me to turn Dad toward me, and I put my arms around him to do so. My cheek was next to his and I whispered, "I love you, Dad." I felt his almost lifeless, huge hand pat me gently twice on the back. Then he slipped into a coma and died a few days later.

Between 1985 and 2007 a lot of water flowed under our family bridges. Some of it sweet and slow but mostly raging torrents!

I want to take you back now to 1990.

CHAPTER 8
Lighting the Blue Touch Paper

In 1990 I wrote to Auntie Rose and asked her if she would get in touch with Janie to see if she would consent to meet me. My aunt was overjoyed and wrote to me to say how much she had longed for this day. She also wrote to Janie, who said she would meet me and would let me have a date soon.

I told Doll and Frank I was thinking of getting in touch with Janie and asked them how would they feel if I did so. Doll said (Frank was silent, as always) that she and Frank would do all they could to support me, "…won't we, Frank?" He nodded in assent.

A few weeks later I got a letter from Auntie Rose saying that Janie's husband objected to her meeting me (I discovered later that he knew nothing of this contact. It had been convenient for Janie to hide behind her husband and say he objected, when, in fact, it was she who was afraid to act) and so she would not go ahead.

I was in the menopausal time of life and perhaps that's why, but I began to bleed after that letter and it did not stop for five years.

I carried on but everything was shot to pieces. Every time I hit a problem of any kind, large or small, Janie would be there in my head, and my heart would have to stretch itself to keep going.

That year Doll and Frank and I went to the island of Kos for a vacation. It was the first time for many years that the three of us had been alone together. Janet, my sister, and Marko had both been invited but both declined.

Apart from Frank's wartime service in the Royal Navy, my parents had hardly traveled abroad in their lives and were like a couple of little birds on the bus from the airport, their heads swiveling 180 degrees as one sunny hotel after the other passed our window. We finally reached our destination—a first-floor apartment in a block right on the beach. They could hardly believe it—it was like heaven.

We had the most wonderful time it is possible to have on a vacation. We never stopped laughing, we explored the locality, Dad got frustrated when he couldn't buy tea bags, we went on boat trips, sat by the crystal-clear, shallow, blue water and read our favorite books. Went to bed when it got dark and got up like three larks at sunrise. Everything was just perfect.

It was to be our swansong and today it brings me great solace to remember it.

By the middle of 1991 I felt my sanity slipping away. I was at home alone one afternoon. Marko had given me some paperwork to do for the natural food business, and I had boxes and boxes of papers to sift through. The more boxes I got through, the more boxes seemed to remain. What was the use of going through all this stupid paper? I had almost forgotten what I was looking for anyway. Why not get rid of it? I took each box and tipped its contents down the stairs. The uncarpeted stairs and landing were covered in two inches of paper.

Next I had to find a box of matches. "Now, where would those be?" There had to be one match in the house somewhere. I ran through the office and bedrooms like a mouse, desperate for that one match. Just strike it once and set the paper alight.

That would do it. No more having to search for the needle in the haystack. My problems would be solved.

I could not find a single match anywhere. After about twenty minutes of the most frantic activity I suddenly stopped.

What was I doing? What was I thinking of? If I set the paper alight the stairs would go up like tinder and I would be trapped upstairs. That would not only be the end of my problems; it would be the end of me! My senses came back and I calmed down. Marko came home and saw the paper strewn all over the house and said not to worry, he would pick it up and re-sort it.

It was cathartic. I wrote again to Auntie Rose and asked if she thought the timing would be good to contact Janie again. She wrote back saying she was going to a family wedding and would mention it to her there.

Janie was at the wedding with her two daughters, and Auntie Rose mentioned it. Janie said no, but her daughters overheard the conversation and insisted that she meet me, for their sakes.

So in January 1992 Marko and I set out for Auntie Rose's house to meet Janie and Chris.

We had stayed at Doll and Frank's the night before and, as usual, when I heard Frank get up to make morning tea I crawled out of my bed and into Doll's. I was excited about the day ahead and wanted to talk it out with her. She was stony and pushed me away. Perhaps I should have expected her to react that way, but I didn't, and the only thing I can say in my own defense is that I was going through quite a tumultuous time emotionally and didn't have the mental energy to look after everyone else's needs. I just told her I loved her. The day had begun and we had to be on our way quite soon. Marko asked Dad for more precise road directions, as he regularly traveled that road, but Dad didn't want to tell him. So we got lost and had to phone Rose from the road.

We finally made it an hour later than scheduled. At last I set eyes on the woman who had brought me into the world. We were like carbon copies of one another. The two of us went for a long walk and talk for four hours, had tea in a seaside café and came back to the house. Janie told me she felt a great weight had lifted off her shoulders now that we had been reunited. We all stayed at Auntie Rose's that night and next day made plans for me to meet my two sisters and brother in a few weeks' time.

Marko and I drove straight up north on the Sunday, to get back to the business for Monday morning. I let the family know what had happened but Doll was far from friendly. I was puzzled but thought she would come around when she realized that my love for her could never diminish. She was my mother and always would be. Not even Janie could take her place in my life.

I couldn't have been more wrong.

In the following weeks there was a call from Doll. How could I do this to her after all she had done for me?! I tried to reason with her—I was not doing anything to her; I was doing something I had to do for myself. She told me I was ungrateful, that she didn't want any more to do with me, and I screamed and put the phone down.

I met my sisters and brother and for the first time ever, when we were sitting together, I realized that I was not making tiny, tiny adjustments inside all the time. I was completely clear and relaxed. So, this is what it feels like to belong.

Doll was intransigent and Frank remained silent. Years

later I asked her why she and my dad and sister had reacted the way they did. "Because you had so much and we had so little," was her reply.

My phone stopped ringing. No more calls from Doll or Janet, my sister. When I called home to London the responses were terse and aggressive. I was completely floored. The price was too high. I could not afford to pay it. I could not live without my lifelong family. I had no choice but to continue to call, to continue to visit, to face the stone wall and meet it head on time after time. They may not have wanted anything to do with me, but I was a member of the family and still wanted—needed—them. I had to persist or die.

Did they not realize, as I did, that to live your life with a set of people forged as strong a bond as shared genes? Doll and Janet were as solid as rocks. They did not budge. My visits home were full of taunts, insults and ridicule. They taught me the truth behind the saying "Blood is thicker than water."

One day, when Janet seemed not quite as furious as usual, I ventured to say to her that she seemed angry about my life. She fixed me with her huge blue eyes and said: "You bet I'm angry. You're the one that got away. I'm stuck with their genes."

After a few years of this I felt like a dead person walking.

I do feel, though, that I should say something about my relationship with Janet, because there is something that weighs heavily on me.

Janet had her own difficulties in childhood and perhaps she will write her own book about that one day. Ill health took her away from home at regular intervals from the age of four until the age of twelve. Every year during that period she left London and its winter smog to go to Sussex by the sea to a place we called "convalescence." This was a beautiful mansion-like building run by the National Health Service to help London children with health issues avoid smog-related disorders. There were many such places, for adults as well as children. My mother used to get on the train every Saturday and go to see her—Frank sometimes used to go, sometimes not. I went a couple of times and was amazed at the beauty of the place, how happy the children were and the pets they had—a donkey, rabbits, chickens, kittens.

When winter was over, Janet would come back to London, go to school and try to pick up her life. But, as she told me years later, she preferred Sussex and never wanted to come home.

Her relations with us at home reflected her disappointment at having to be with us again. She was what they called "difficult" and I remember her being at the center of lots of family arguments. I would take her side most of the time, not just because I adored her, but because I also realized how difficult it must have been for her to switch from one place to the other. I was puzzled, too, by my parents' attitude toward her reckless behavior. They seemed helpless before her and unable to guide or control her. I asked Doll what was her own difficulty with regulating Janet. After all, I said, if I had done any one of those things she would not have hesitated to clip me around the ear. Doll went quiet and looked at the floor. "What's the matter, Mum?" I asked. "Margaret, don't make me say it." "Say what?" "She is my daughter," said Doll. "And so am I your daughter," said I, not daring to allow Doll's remark to sink in.

It was not until Janet was in her early twenties that she confided in me that she, too, had been sexually abused—by Doll's brother, Brian (Brian was married to Ruby, Frank's sister)—when she was five years old. She tried to describe her experience to me but gagged on her words about halfway through. Her distress about it was acute, and I would notice ever afterward that when Brian's name was mentioned a cloud would cross her face and she would look downcast. We both kept the inevitable silence. I did try to explain it once to Janet's two daughters when they were angry with their mother's behavior toward them and, I felt, adult enough to take the information in without being harmed by it, but they both responded in the same way. They stared at me and tried hard to disbelieve it, but I feel they knew I was telling the truth, because they occasionally mention it. I think it is really very difficult for people to know how to respond to such news. The atmosphere around such topics becomes very awkward as people struggle to know what to say. What does one say? "Oh! I didn't know" or "Oh, really?" I withheld the name of the abuser because I felt I had to consider the feelings of Brian's son, Marcus. The web of deceit always tightens around one's neck.

When Janet was twelve and I twenty there was a real fracas at home just as I was about to leave to go to Robbie's house. Frank and Doll, Kitty, Janet and I were in the living room and Janet was the subject of discontent. She had been pretty wild this time and I was beginning to worry that there was really something quite deep going wrong with her. Frank and Doll—or really Doll—seemed to be at a loss and kept saying the same things over and over, and Janet became more and more insolent.

I felt my temper rising to the surface as she told our parents how much she hated living with them. "What about me?" I asked. "I like living with you," she said. "Why?" I challenged.

"Because you are my sister."

May God forgive me for what I said next…

"Well, I'm not your sister," said I.

Janet came to a full stop. Her mouth dropped open. Silence from her at last.

In a raging temper I told Janet that I was adopted and not her sister, so there, she didn't know everything about us!

Doll cried out, "Oh no! She's told her, she's told her!" and ran into her bedroom.

Then, after giving this child the shock of her life, I promptly left to go to Robbie's.

I did to Janet the very same thing that had been done to me at her age: I pulled out the rug from under her feet. And just as I rejected the person who did it to me, Janet ultimately rejected me.

In the coming years we were to have a long period of being close, but I believe the resentment was too big for us in the end. When family relationships were challenged again, Janet went for my jugular without a moment's hesitation.

If I could take back only one thing in my life that I regretted and nullify it, it would be that.

I know Frank had that same feeling about his abuse of me.

Perhaps Martin, the man who had told me that neither of my parents were my own, also felt regret. He was a great loss in my life. He was from the Republic of Ireland and his girlfriend, Maisie, worked with Doll and needed somewhere to live. Doll said she could stay with us and she did for about a year before she and Martin got married. It was cheaper for her to stay with us and share the family costs, rather than pay for the upkeep of a whole apartment of her own, and Doll was intentionally giving them a helping hand toward the wedding.

During that year Maisie, Martin and I became very close. I was twelve years old and they began taking me out and about with them to the movies, etc. and I had a lot of fun with them. Martin, especially, and I would have long, long talks about my potential and what I might like to be when I grew up; we talked about everything under the sun and spent many happy hours together. He became a man I knew I could trust and I looked forward to the outings with him and Maisie.

All that came to a sudden stop. No more thrilling conversations, no more outings. By this time I was good at bearing disappointment, but I wondered why the sudden silence. Then one weekend Martin managed to take me aside and tell me that Doll had forbidden him to have anything to do with me. My relationship with him was upsetting Frank and it had to stop. The fact that Frank and I had never had a decent conversation must have hit home at last.

Pretty soon after that huge slice of injustice pie had been administered, Martin and Maisie got married. I was chief bridesmaid and they moved into their tiny apartment in a very old tenement. I saw them occasionally on my way home from school and would call in at weekends at their invitation now and then.

One Saturday when I dropped in, Martin took me into their dark little living room and sat me down. He started talking about Doll and Frank and, after quite a few minutes, he asked me if I could guess what he was trying to tell me. I was completely perplexed and said no. Martin looked very sad. Maisie had come into the room to be with us and they both looked quiet and sorry about something. Martin put his hand on my shoulder and said, "You're adopted, Marg."

It's hard to describe what happened next, because nothing is the reality of it. I behaved as though nothing had happened. After a while I left and got on the bus to go home. I remember sitting on the top deck of the bus but don't remember what was going through my mind. I did what I had always done—I just carried on.

Through my own decision, I lost two of the most beautiful people there have ever been in my life. I just could not face seeing them again. A few years later they moved away. I think they had three children. Martin died at age fifty during surgery.

Worse is yet to come with this story. I have picked up hints over the years that Doll had asked Martin to tell me I was adopted. I'm sure Martin thought he would be able to put it across in a gentle manner that I would be able to take from someone I loved so much. I believe he did what he felt was the best thing to do. Doll, however, was shrewd enough to know what the news would do to me. She dealt the final blow to a relationship she and Frank were jealous of.

> *I am on a small boat on a very rough sea. Strewn on the deck are three body bags. I know that one is Doll, one is Frank and the third is Janet. The boat is in danger and there is only me alive. I have to get rid of the bodies. I drag the largest bag, Frank, to the edge of the boat and with a lot of heaving and sweating manage to get the bag half over the hand rail with the waves breaking over the boat and the boat teetering over the sharp waves. There he is, my father, half on and half off the boat, and I am going to heave*

> *him over the side into the raging sea. I look around me—*
> *at the other two bags waiting to meet the same fate. This*
> *can't be right. They can't really be dead. They've just stopped*
> *breathing for a while. I can't ditch them forever. With a lot*
> *more sweating and heaving I manage to drag Frank back*
> *onto the boat. That's better. They're not going into the sea. I'll*
> *keep them until they start breathing again.*

It took me twenty years to reach an understanding of what this vision may have been about. That fact tells me a lot about how I was during that time. The vision occurred just after I had met Janie, my birth mother, her husband and my two stepsisters and stepbrother.

This vision of the body bags on the boat tells me very clearly that my relationships with my adoptive parents and sister are over. Dead. It also addresses my inability to accept this. I choose to hang on to their remains and wait out the storm in the hope that the relationships will breathe again someday. The message is very clear but I did not dare face this truth while the storm was raging.

But my quantum self knew the truth and sent me a message that, though I could not accept it on the surface level, helped prepare me to face the facts when I was ready. It was a lifesaver.

The reactions of my adoptive family to my having made contact with my birth family knocked me for a loop. I simply could not believe that they would do the exact opposite of what they had promised they would do! Doll had assured me, with

Frank's assent, that they would support me if I should contact Janie. Their vitriol was like something wild and awful that had been suddenly unleashed. They stood like stone statues in the room when I was present. They said nothing to me and responded with a clipped "Yes" or "No" to any comments I ventured. When I did catch their eye they would stare unblinkingly, their mouths would become thin slits and their skin would blench. Janet was verbally abusive about my appearance and about anything I said, and she looked as though she could become violent at any moment. But none of them ever said anything about Janie or the issue of my adoption. They behaved as though I didn't exist, as though I was not really there.

It was just too much for me to take in. "They'll get over it soon," I thought. And I really believed they would. Nothing around me helped me understand what was going on. Their rage was irrational, unreasonable, primitive.

Within a year of meeting Janie and Chris and the huge extended family, everything that confirmed my identity in this everyday life, beginning in 1945 and up to that moment in 1992 when I met my birth mother, had gone, swept away by the tide: my marriage to Marko, our business, the lucrative second career I had as a management trainer, my adoptive family, my health, my home, my anticipated future. There suddenly appeared to be a huge financial debt that Marko and I were responsible for without the means to repay. It felt like a meltdown and I found myself doing some things that were uncharacteristic of me. I lost my way for a while, saw myself keeping company with people that were not good for me. I left Marko. My life seemed to spin out of control and there was no solid person or ground to set me straight.

After about a year of free fall I finally got sick. All energy left me and even to get out of bed was too much of a struggle sometimes. My body seemed to come to a full stop. I did get to consult a neurologist at a hospital in Liverpool, who told me that it was not the onset of a crippling disease and that my energy would come back one day. That probably qualifies as the best news I have ever had in my life, but I accepted it with a shrug. My ability to care about anything was seriously impaired. It was to be six years before I was able to live a full life again.

I said nothing about being sick to either family. I used to struggle to make visits and behave as normal, but Janie seemed suspicious around me, and Doll once said, "You've got that ME, you have." ME is myalgic encephalomyelitis, better known as chronic fatigue syndrome.

Doll was always one to speak out the things others would not dare say. This was both a saving grace and a huge drawback, I suppose. I loved it—even when I was on the receiving end!

For example, a gentleman came to see us once. He had a huge, red, glowing boil on the end of his nose. There were about four of us there and we chatted about this and that, all trying desperately to ignore the boil.

After an hour or so, it was growing dark and I got up to turn on the light. "Don't bother with the light, Margaret. His nose is throwing enough of it out to light up the room," commanded Doll.

I could have died. I felt so bad for the poor man and yet couldn't think of anything to say to take away the embarrassment. I seem to remember that I didn't turn the light on, and that must have added injury to insult!

Six decades of this interesting character trait of Doll's

trained me to discriminate between the times when it was of service and those when it was not. It was she who told me when I had a run in my stockings or a blemish on my face, and her method of delivery was that of a sergeant major on the parade ground. But she also alerted me to traits in my own character that obviously annoyed her and so might have annoyed others also. Her running commentary on my ugly knees and spotty face, rather than reduce me to ashes, only served to draw my attention to those parts of me and force me to assess if what she had said was really worth taking some action on. In the case of the spots, I stopped eating sugar for about fifteen years—that had to be good! The knees…well, they sorted themselves out once I was through puberty.

I clung to Doll as one who is drowning clings to a rock. She didn't like it and would frequently push me away—and once she physically did just that. It was a Saturday morning and I was twelve years old. Doll had been browbeating and trashing me since I got up, and I was so traumatized I fainted. I was out for the count for a while and when I came to I saw her looking down at me and frowning. In my despair I held out my arms to her: "Mummy, Mummy, please!" I tried to put my arms around her but there was no blood in my head and I was flailing. I felt her fury as she literally swiped my arms away from her and then gripped my arms tightly, rendering them useless—it was a fight and I was half in and half out of it. To this day I have no idea what I did to warrant such violence from her, but I can guess that it was something that cut her very deeply—like Frank's frequent philandering with other women.

In day-to-day life I never knew which barb she was going to throw out next, and sometimes I would laugh so hard she had no alternative but to share the joke. It was very good training in how to refuse to take offense.

When the boot was on the other foot, however, it was a different thing. Any look or remark, however innocent, that she perceived as a criticism of her would have her flying into a rage and sending a torrent of insults to her abuser. She only accepted the nice things said about her, and that was good enough for me. I wanted her to be happy. After all, something in her life must have hurt her very deeply to make her like that. She had plenty of pain material.

When I look back to that time of my meltdown I see, with the luxury of hindsight, that everything that was not real in my life was swept away at once. That is to say, everything I had worked so hard to build on the foundation of nods, winks and whispers—my house built on sand—collapsed like a set of cards. I was then forty-seven years old. I was to continue for another twelve or so years trying to rebuild on the basis of the old model—another city, another marriage—but nothing worked for long. Only when I realized that my life is about something else altogether and followed that new star did things start to fall into place.

Back in 1993, however, and not for the first time, I stood alone, at the top of the flagpole, with nothing but space around me. Had I known that this collapse of my life would endure for more than twenty years, with a brief period of respite after twelve, followed by more of the same, I'm not sure what I would have done. Thank goodness for lack of knowledge.

But, I forget, I did have knowledge. Knowledge of the absolute truth of life that came to me from out of the blue and never failed me.

> *I am sitting with a large group of people practicing my daily meditation. I open my eyes slightly. There, about three feet in front of me, is a huge, huge rock, tapered at the top and wide at the bottom. I close my eyes. Open them. The rock is still there. I close my eyes again. Now the rock is inside me. It fills my body completely and my skin is stretched around it. I am a millimeter or two bigger than the rock.*
>
> *It's going to be heavy to move through life. It will be a close thing. But I am the bigger of the two. I will survive it.*

This vision occurred about a year after my moorings in life had been severed by my adoptive family's rage. I was about to buckle under the strain and struggle against severe fatigue for six years.

This experience was so graphic there was no avoiding its positive message. Yes, it was going to be huge. It was going to be hard and heavy. But I would take it in and contain it. There was a price and I was going to pay it, but I would survive.

I needed nothing else to keep me going.

From 1993 to 1999—the years of my incapacity due to what was never officially diagnosed but which was referred to by health professionals as "fatigue"—I continued knocking on Doll and Frank's door. I was never naive enough to expect any change in the emotional temperature, but I was not going to be shoved aside and forgotten just because it was easier for them to

82

do that than to approach the issue like rational human beings. I waited and hoped. Janet's rage became a fire that blazes still today, but Doll's did begin to cool. One weekend in 1995, when Doll's frozen rigidity had been particularly hard to take, I left the house to go to an appointment and said "Goodbye, Mum" as I quietly left. I was just about to turn the corner that would take me out of sight of the apartment, when I heard Doll call my name. I looked back and there she was, standing outside the street door waving a dish towel. I waved back and carried on walking. I felt no emotion except a small glimmer of hope. Hope that this was a breakthrough. And it was. She began to bend.

CHAPTER 9
More Silence

Doll's attitude softened in 1995 and she said she would allow me back but I was forbidden to speak of anything that was important to me—meditation, my beliefs, my birth family, my childhood. She just did not want to know.

This meant that every time I visited "home" I left most of myself on the mat outside the street door.

I respected her wishes so well that I believe she came to regret she ever made those terms. At a family wedding in 2002 a much-loved cousin sat with our little group. He was known for saying the things most people kept quiet about, so he was a lot of fun! He said he felt that my mother really wanted to know what was going on between me and my birth family and that I should just talk about it with her.

I replied that I would continue to respect her wishes and that if she really wanted to know, she would not be shy about asking me—she had, after all, not been shy about imposing her draconian restrictions. I felt bound by them. It was up to her to change them.

You can call that revenge if you like—it was, a bit.

The years passed by. I kept visiting home and we began to have a little fun sometimes. I would stay for a month or two at times to try to ease the burden on Doll of constant caring for Frank, who now had Parkinson's disease.

When I had left home in 1966 to marry Robbie, Doll had

been on the threshold of the menopause, in her early forties. It was not an easy time for her, and her doctor prescribed Valium. She was on that drug for several years until her severe insomnia led the same doctor to prescribe Mogadon, a much stronger drug that would literally "knock her out" when she took it at bedtime.

Belonging to the family of benzodiazepines, central nervous system depressants, a sedative hypnotic drug, Mogadon is now only allowed to be prescribed to any individual for a maximum of six weeks, so I was told by one of the organizations that deal with drugs and drug addiction on an everyday basis. Doll lived to be ninety-two and was on Mogadon for all that time—more than forty-five years! Officially, she would have been considered an "involuntary drug addict." She made several attempts to come off it—even filing a little off each tablet night after night—but soon reverted to the full dosage. She just could not cope without it, could not sleep or cope with life's little things. She became so aggressive without it that it was impossible to be around her for any length of time. In other words, she became addicted to prescribed drugs. It was a very serious matter and one that we did not, at that time, understand the implications of. Today, benzodiazepine addiction is considered even more dangerous than dependence on opioids.

In 2007 Frank died. Doll was just not interested in fun from then on. In fact, I think I never saw her smile after he left. There was a big thing about his ashes. I kept reminding Janet and Doll by telephone to go and collect them. (I lived elsewhere in Europe from 2005 until 2008, when I moved to America, making frequent trips home to visit both families until 2011, the year that my relationship with Doll and Janet finally collapsed.) They finally got to the crematorium a day before there was to have been a random scattering of his ashes. They brought the urn home and, when I visited them soon after that, the dresser in the sitting room had become a shrine to Dad, with photos, etc. and the urn in the middle.

The next time I went home the urn was on the window ledge behind the curtain, and by my third visit it was in the bottom of the closet in the spare bedroom!

Doll did well with her aging. She looked after herself with care and always looked clean and neat. I spoke to her most days from my base in Holland and still took time to travel to England and spend long periods with her, when I did most of the running around and all the cooking.

As far as my extended adoptive family was concerned, the ones I had been so happy with when we first moved to the East End, there were very few occasions when I met them and talked about my origins with them. Those who knew had been sworn to secrecy and had kept their vow for the love of me—a very different thing from the other kind of secrecy I had experienced as the nods and winks and whispers. The first occasion the question of my birth and adoption came up was the wedding in 2002 when my cousin suggested I just ignore Doll's ban and talk to her about my birth family. Most of Frank's family were there, and Ruby and Brian's son, Marcus, my closest cousin, had confirmation for the first time on that day that I was the family's adopted child and he was very distressed. He is two years younger than me, and he and my uncle Dave—eight months younger than me—and I had spent a lot of time together as children, there in the East End street with the green door. Marcus knew that someone in the family had been adopted but not who it was. His first thought was to make me financially secure by giving me half his business. He said he wanted to be a brother to me. I told him he didn't need to do that, that I couldn't possibly love him more even if he were my brother. He stopped midsentence, looked me straight in the eyes, threw his arms around me and planted a huge kiss on my face. I will never forget that. What a gem!

The second occasion was in June 2013, a year after the final collapse of my relationship with Doll and Janet, when that same uncle, Dave—another priceless gem in my life—told me that my sister Janet had rung round to everyone individually in January 2012 and said that Doll's instruction to them was that they should all shun me. No explanation. I had upset her and that was all they needed to know. Apparently they had each listened to the instruction, put the phone down and then come out strongly in my support.

Frank's many brothers and sisters had all known Doll for six decades. They had known me, also, since I was a year old. Nobody was going to tell them how to vote. That was such a light in my darkness! Like a lighthouse scanning the dark waters and saving souls. Saving my soul. All of those people had shown me love all my life, and still do—those that are still on the planet. It's almost worth going through something like this, because when you find a friend you know they are yours for life.

CHAPTER 10

Loose Ends

It is February 2010 and I have traveled from the US to live in Holland for a while. As I move around I am aware of a tugging at my skirts. I look and there is nothing there, but the feeling persists and for some reason I keep thinking of Robbie, whom I have not seen for thirty-five years.

I contact Robbie's niece Lottie and ask her how he is doing. I tell her he is tugging at my skirts and wants some attention. There is no response from Lottie, which is unusual, and I think it must be nothing...I must have been mistaken. In August I hear from Lottie. In February Robbie had experienced severe pain in his legs but had avoided consulting his doctor. By now the cancer had spread, he was in hospital. Lottie and her husband had been to see him and on the surface he seemed very well and cheerful.

Robbie was the last person I would want in my life after all this time. It is sobering to realize, through this vision, that close relationships do not necessarily end with divorce or walking away. Robbie had had a succession of women in his life since we split up and three adored children with his second wife. When he felt vulnerable his inner self flew back to me to let me know, as though no time had passed since we last met. His instinct took him back to the beginning, back to me.

Those deep bonds between people outlast time and space. It is the love, I think, that lasts. Everything else falls away. The legal stuff does not have the same eternal grip.

I was due to visit the UK in August and September 2010 and, as usual, set about making arrangements to meet up with Lottie and her husband, Bob, and Ellie and husband, Damien. Lottie and Damien were the niece and nephew of Robbie.

When I left Robbie in 1976 I said nothing to anyone about what had happened between us. His mother and Damien's mother—her daughter and Robbie's sister—rejected me outright and refused to see me again. They were a powerful lobby in the family and the children (who were by now all married) stayed in the background. However, Lottie wrote to me a few years later and said she didn't care what they thought anymore, she wanted to have contact with me and would I write to her. I was delighted. I missed all the family dreadfully—we had had so much fun together.

When Damien heard Lottie and I were in touch he said he wanted to see me again. The first time the five of us met up, Damien was shaking as he greeted me and his breath was coming in quick gasps. He had been ten years old when he and I first met and I was fifteen—a huge age gap at that time of life. For Damien I was one of those first loves that are never forgotten. I had never realized this, but after several meetings with them over the years I saw that his attachment to me was very strong—even though he was blissfully happily married and even when a grandfather. His love for me was so beautiful—so full of awe and respect and so openly shared with the others in joy—that I responded with tenderness while feeling very special.

In September 2010 I was in London staying with Doll and due to meet Ellie and Damien that evening. Lottie and her husband, Bob, were unable to make it. We made plans to meet at Canary Wharf, but I got the location wrong and we almost missed one another. It was thanks to Doll's ingenuity and cell phones that we managed to track one another down and I finally got to the proper spot to see Damien running toward me, arms outstretched.

It was late by this time and many of the restaurants were closing. We managed to find some coffee and a sheltered place to sit and started to catch up with one another.

Robbie was the prime subject of our conversation. That day, Damien said, he had been moved to a hospice. I felt myself melt inside. Thirty-five years and something was still alive in there.

We began to talk about life and death and the huge events in everyone's lives. Gently, very gently, the subject turned to what had happened between Robbie and me. They had never brought the subject up before. Ellie said they had all known that it must have been something very serious for me to walk away. God bless her for saying that!

I gave them a few details and finished with the sex at the party. I was shaking by this time and Damien took a sharp intake of breath. He and Ellie were shocked by what I told them. I had never mentioned it to anyone before that night and it set me wobbling like a jelly inside.

Everything around us was closed and shuttered when we set out for their car and they took me to Doll's house. Damien was always a little tearful when we parted. I felt so lucky to have such a strong and innocent love in my life.

The next day Damien called me at Doll's. Robbie had had a stroke in the morning and passed away, with his three children by his side, at 2:30 p.m. Damien didn't feel inclined to attend the funeral, given what I had told him the night before. I said that his Uncle Robbie had loved him very much and that Damien needed to think of his own relationship with Robbie and not of mine. He should go ahead. He said he would and we hung up.

I was full of self-doubt. Why, after thirty-five years of silence, did I have to tell Robbie's family the night before he died?

Little did I know. Little did I know.

And now, today, I think about that night. The last night I was to see Damien, who passed away himself in 2017, on Midsummer's Day, June 21, after a two-week illness.

It is the day before Robbie's funeral in 2010 and I am leaving London to return to Holland, where I have been on an extended stay from the US. A driver from the local cab company comes to pick me up at Doll's and take me to the Eurostar terminal at St. Pancras station, near Kings Cross.

The traffic is just awful and we get stuck for quite a while. The driver tells me he has another job and that he will be going up north later that day. I am less interested than I would usually be and just respond with "Hmmm."

Then he tells me about his other job. He is a medium. I do not welcome this news and feel trapped inside the cab surrounded by half of London's traffic.

My sister Janet had been plagued throughout child- and adulthood with visions of dead people. For years she and I had talked about what was happening to her—it seemed that I was able to give her an interpretation of what her experiences meant (Janet knew nothing of my own history of visions). After some pretty hair-raising run-ins with departed souls who were not happy and seemed bent on revenge, I took Janet by the hand one day and we went to the College of Psychic Studies in London. By the time that day arrived I had dead people riding on my back and hanging from every limb. I had had enough. The lady at the college was very honest with us, saying that they did not know anything about the realms they were dealing with. However, after Janet had been interviewed by one of their consultants, she was told that she had been born a medium. This answered so many questions for her that she began to relax a little, although the visitations were still pretty scary, with Janet taking risks that I did not want to be involved with. When she began socializing with the seedy side of local life I backed off and wished her luck. All her playing around with energies that we did not understand warned me off ever getting involved with that level of life again.

"In fact, there are some people here for you," said Keith the cabbie. Oh, Lordy, here we go, I thought. Then Keith proceeded to tell me details of Janie and her sister Lucy, both deceased, and how they had been watching me during this visit to London. He told me what they had seen and it was perfectly accurate.

"And there is someone else here…" He gave me some details that I quickly put together as Damien's father, Chas, Robbie's brother-in-law. "And 'Arry's with me," said Chas (through Keith). That made me sit up. The connections were becoming uncanny. Harry was Robbie's brother. "And Robbie's here with us." I fell back in the seat and quickly sat up again. "He said to tell you that his legs don't hurt anymore. He's fine. And by the way, we're all going to be on the train with you to Holland."

Everything went misty. The next thing I knew we were pulling up outside St. Pancras. Keith got out and helped me with my luggage. By this time I thought of him as a dear friend. I looked at him and saw a sweet man who had some kind of gift.

As we were about to part, Keith said to me that he knew it sounded fresh but Robbie wanted him to kiss me—would that be all right. I said yes it would and offered my cheek. Keith leaned forward and kissed my cheek. It wasn't Keith. It was Robbie.

This gave me a taste of how it is to receive messages "from the other side."

It felt absolutely nothing like the feelings that accompany my visions. I do not doubt at all the honesty and good intentions of Keith the cabbie, and everything he conveyed to me from departed relatives was completely accurate. But this was an interaction with people who were existing at some level that lacked unity. That's how it felt, anyway. There was no feeling of bliss, of strength, of a knowingness that surpassed that of everyday life. In fact, it was more like everyday life itself, with its relationships continuing on some other level. I have the feeling the level of life tapped into here was authentic yet somehow unfinished and therefore carrying some stress. It seems natural for those there to want to communicate with remembered loved ones. Evidence of life's continuum. I can understand how it would bring comfort to those grieving. We need to know that they are still around, perhaps. And perhaps they need us to know the very same. It didn't feel at all spooky. I cannot pretend to know anything about this kind of experience other than what I felt at the time and have outlined here.

My visit home in late 2010 proved to be a turning point for other reasons. Doll seemed totally committed to destructive behavior and I was her lightning rod. One afternoon, at the kitchen table, she lit into me with a stream of abuse about what a "big mouth" I had and how I couldn't be trusted with any information, I was such a loudmouth as a kid and an adult. The straw broke the camel's back! I told her very quietly that she was wrong…That I had, in fact, been silent for more than fifty-five years in order to protect her and the family unit…That she should keep silence herself and never call me a loudmouth. She wanted to know what I had kept silent about.

I told her that a member of the family had treated me badly throughout my childhood and I had kept quiet about it in order to keep the peace. How badly? she asked. They had been violent, I said.

Doll was quiet for twenty-four hours. Then she called my niece Grace, the younger of Janet's two daughters, who lived very close by and who was pregnant with her first child. Doll asked me to repeat what I had told her in front of Grace, which I did. Doll was losing face and she didn't like it. She was aggressive and angry. She obviously did not want to believe it but she didn't call me a liar.

Grace was wonderful. The fact that it was Frank was hanging in the air between us. He was an adored grandfather, neighbor and member of the community he and Doll lived in.

I had no intention of telling Doll who it was or the true extent of the abuse. I felt it would have been just too much for her.

I walked Grace home and she was sweetness itself, but saddened by the accusations. As we parted I said to her that Doll's reaction made me think that I would have to "go"—that Doll would not want me around anymore. Grace closed her eyes and nodded.

I said it was no wonder that young children kept things quiet if this could happen between mature adults. Grace said she felt that Doll was capable of absorbing the information and behaving constructively with it. Capable she may have been, but I knew from Grace's nod that she believed, as I did, that Doll would not handle this information well.

The last time I saw Doll was late in 2011. She was eighty-nine years old. Janie, Chris and Frank were all gone. I stayed with her for a couple of months after an accident that broke many bones in her face. Allopathic medicine told her it could do nothing and she should get used to the nerve pain, but we found a good massage therapist who did the most gentle work on her face with oils, and the pain disappeared. But she was cranky and furious by this time, and I couldn't do a thing right.

The massage therapist offered her acupuncture one day after a treatment session, saying she thought it would help with any residual nerve pain. Doll was hesitant—even going for massage had broken her boundaries. I said why didn't she try it, that I had had some acupuncture in the past and it had helped and the process didn't hurt. She turned her head to look straight at me. Her face was cold with fury. "You!" she said. "You! Nothing hurts you! It would take a bullet!" She spat out the words.

So that was it. All this time she had been so busy driving stakes into my heart that she had been distracted from the anguish on my face. If you ever come up against this yourself, I recommend that you prewrap your heart in cling wrap or, better still, that film you can get from Amazon for electronic devices that covers fragile glass and makes it strong. Then, the next time some maniac takes a hammer to it, it won't shatter into a million pieces. They will, of course, tell you how hard-hearted you are, but c'est la vie—at least you will still be standing and free. Free to whisper to the wind, to fly with eagles and swim with the tides. That's what's important.

Doll spent a lot of time sabotaging my efforts to get her to eat a good meal. The warden and some of her friends in the retirement complex she had lived in for the last fifteen years approached me and said they were convinced she was anorexic. The warden had seen it before in the elderly. I began to think Doll needed someone with her on a permanent basis. Before I could bring the subject up to her, she told me she didn't want anyone to live with her, she wanted to be alone. I countered by saying I felt she needed someone with her for a while longer.

She wanted rid of me and did everything she could think of to drive me away. She was such an unhappy, depressed, angry old lady.

It all came to a head in December 2011 when her cruelty reached new depths and I said I had had enough, I was leaving and not coming back. Janet came round (a rare visit). I was shaking with rage and told them both that it was time for the abuse to stop. Janet took Doll home with her.

In my heart I had known for years—perhaps since I was eight and had held my baby sister in my arms—that when I made my first mistake it would be my last. I had never known either Doll or Janet to forgive anyone a perceived transgression. And this was a big one. And anyway, they needed it to be my fault. Like all true hypocrites, they clung to the moral high ground.

I spent the night at my own point of no return. No matter how many times I reach this point—and I've reached it quite a few times so far—it never gets easier. I was rock solid within myself: clear and strong. I had come to the point where a decision had to be made and I had made it. The thing I had dreaded most for all my life was now upon me: the loss of Doll as my mother. That night I faced the cruelest pain I had ever imagined. And yet my path was crystalline. I understood very well the implications of this latest action of mine. By walking away from her I was going to assume full responsibility for all the bad feeling, all the anger, all the distress.

But that was nothing new. That was what I had always done. Frank's first remembered abuse when I was eight had thrust a terrible, lonely responsibility on my shoulders. The harmony or dysfunction of the family unit had rested on my responses since then. As long as I kept quiet about it and carried my crushing burden without bothering anyone else with my feelings, things could carry on as though nothing had happened. That is what I had done for more than fifty-five years until suddenly, one day, I had broken my silence. How dare I do that! What a terrible thing to do to one's own family! To break the pact. My, how they would make me suffer for that.

So it worked itself out that way. To the people driven mad by their own anger I am the villain of the piece. I am cut off as though dead with no mention of my name—and I no longer have to live with their hostility. What a relief!

And I accept full responsibility for all the events leading up to that last night at my mother's apartment in the retirement complex. If I had not been in the family, these terrible things might not have happened. Who knows what it must have been like to live with my "silence" for all those years? Those of us who have lived with these things know that hidden feelings seep through the cracks and make themselves felt somehow. That's what I had picked up as a very young child—their hidden feelings seeping through the cracks. Truth is a magnificent thing. It will not be abused all the time. It has a habit of coming out when we least expect it. It is always a healing thing, even though it may tear us to pieces: better to live with a cruel truth than a comfortable lie. That night I opted for the cruel truth and have been living with it ever since.

Truth and I. We are partners. My existence is evidence of the truth of my birth mother's actions. For her, to look at me was to look at her own shame. For Frank, facing my anger was having to face up to the truth of his own vileness. Who wants to do that on a regular basis? And for Doll—how heartbreaking for both of us—I was a constant reminder of the baby that had died. "There's never a day goes by without my thinking of her," Doll had said on that fateful night. That had been one of those statements that seemed to burst out of her in the last few days I was to spend with her. They were awful truths that carried some kind of liberation with them, as though she were able, just for a moment, to get close enough to herself to speak with clarity. She would suddenly say, "For years I've watched you tearing yourself apart," and then, "I've always been mental. Yes, I have."

Better to be the abused than the abuser. Better to be the

evidence than the shame. Is this really true? Or is it some dastardly trick of nature to make us believe that being good is what is right? I see victims of abuse being publicly pilloried all the time. Do those babies that come out of the blue without the proper paperwork and those that have to endure abuse have any chance of making it to some level of decency, while those who commit the atrocities live as though decent? Is it really true that once we do something that we are ashamed of we lose the light at the end of the tunnel?

People seem to be very good indeed at building themselves a defense system in order to maintain an acceptable persona. Offer up the child and pretend it never happened and let that child live out the terror. At least then you can start again— another chance…Just make sure it doesn't happen again. Get rid of the evidence and nobody will know what happened. You can then be decent again. Who cares what happens to the evidence? Accuse the abused of abuse when they speak out the truth, and turn the victim into a criminal. Whatever happens, don't accept responsibility for your own unacceptable actions, for that will be the death of your reputation, and reputation is all.

Fine as a strategy. Except that it doesn't work in the long run. Life only requires us to know our own shame ourselves for the whole process of guilt to continue. But for now, as long as our own actions can be buried we may as well continue with them. If the social rigors of the day heap shame upon us for some of the things we do and force desperate measures upon people when at their most vulnerable, then perhaps we have to ask the question, "Who is paying the price here?"

Oh no! Don't ask that. I can't bear it. The answer's always the same: the children.

The first thing I did next morning was meditate. I needed to be feeling strong inside to get through this coming day.

While I was meditating, Doll, Janet and her fiancé arrived. They were quick and quiet as they moved around Doll's apartment. I heard Doll say, "Margaret, it's us," followed by "Oh, let's be quick, be quick." She had left something vital behind and they had to come to retrieve it. I continued meditating yet felt in the presence of burglars. Doll's voice had sounded frightened. Anger from her I was used to and could take on the chin. But her fear was too much for me to bear. It was the killer blow. Any dream I may have entertained that things might be harmonious again between her and me dissolved into the morning air. My mother was afraid of me. I had to melt away.

I packed my things and was gone by midafternoon. While organizing my things to leave, I found I needed to change a twenty-pound note for two ten-pound notes. Doll always kept a glass tumbler in her china cabinet stuffed full of paper money. I had counted it out for her one day and told her there was £450 in the tumbler and wouldn't it be a good idea to put it in the bank? She flatly refused and said she'd rather leave it where it was. I went to the tumbler with my twenty-pound note in my hand to get the change I needed. It was empty. They had taken the money that morning. I stared at the tumbler in disbelief. I think that was the worst moment of all—the realization that they thought I might steal Doll's money. Whenever I think of it my shoulders start to shake involuntarily.

The injustice of that act by them could have me frothing at the mouth. It might have had some credibility had it been the other way around.

The feeling of having been robbed has been familiar to

me all my life. Entering into any financial arrangement with members of my immediate family always confirmed that feeling and made it concrete. As it is, I will never have the opportunity to tell them what they robbed me of that morning and I just have to learn to live a good life in spite of it. It took all the issues between us forever away from any level of humanitarianism, of decency, of reason, of hope and dumped them into a slimy pit of human filth. When it came down to it, they used money to tell me I was worthless to them. It was very clever really. If they wanted to ensure that I would never get to the top of Everest intact they succeeded brilliantly.

Yet again I was out on the street with nowhere to go. I went and stayed serially with friends for a while before going back to the USA in February. I had never been so low in spirits. I felt done for, guilty for walking away from my mother, and homeless.

Six months later I returned to England and sent a message to Doll that I was there and would she like to see me. I really did not want to have to live with such bad feeling in my life and so I swallowed my pride once again. I would have liked there to have been friendliness between us, with an acceptance of the fact that there were issues that may never be resolved. But Doll had found her resolution. The answer came back: "No." Janet and her older daughter have both written me off. Janet knew about the abuse from Frank—not because I told her but because she had asked me one day if he had ever "touched me" and I said yes. She categorically denied that he had ever done the same to her, and I believed her.

Grace is Janet's younger daughter and is one of my stalwarts. She has seen things with her own eyes and comes to her own conclusions. It pains me to think of ruining any hopes she may have that it was not her grandfather who was responsible for the terrible secret violence, and we never discuss it. Silence again. Still hidden after all these years. But now comes a book! One day, perhaps, I will be able to stand the thought of losing Grace, but not yet, not yet. Truth, please wait for me awhile. In the meantime, she and I love one another very much—she spent a lot of time with me and Marko as a child—and she is my lifeline to my old family. A very precious human being, honest and smart.

In January 2015 I heard from a couple of sources that Doll was failing. She was at home with Janet and her new husband. I was in the USA and was not considered relevant by either Doll or Janet. So I kept in touch via third parties.

The day came when Grace told me that Doll could not lift her head and was not eating or drinking. I told Grace that I thought it would be just a matter of days now and that I'd like to write a goodbye message to Doll. Would she take it to her for me and read it to her? She said of course she would, it would be a nice thing to do.

I wrote the message that afternoon and had the distinct feeling that someone was looking over my shoulder while I composed it. I sent the finished message by email to Grace.

She got to Janet's house two hours after Doll died. She sat alone with Doll's body for some minutes and then said to her, "Nan, I'm going to read a message to you from Margaret." It may seem a strange thing to do, to speak and read to a dead body, but if you have been in the presence of a departed loved one you, too, may feel that in some sense they are "still there" for a while.

She started to read it and soon began to cry. She apologized to Doll and said she would begin again.

"Do you know, Marg," Grace said, "it felt as though Nan said—"

I interrupted her. "Nan said to you, 'Don't bother, I know what it says—I've read it already.'"

"Yes, how did you know?" asked Grace, stupefied.

"Because she was here with me when I was writing it," I said. So, my feeling had been vindicated: there had been someone looking over my shoulder. A last visit from Doll before leaving.

Dearest Mum

When I was a little girl there sometimes were days when you seemed to have had enough of the world and would take to your bed. My world seemed to come to a complete stop on those days and I just waited for you to get back to your normal self as quickly as possible. Your normal self was to be in complete command of the household, on top of all the jobs that needed to be done and with tons and tons of energy at your disposal.

This is the first time I have known you to take to your bed for more than a day at a time. This means that the world stopped turning some weeks ago. I am supposed to be old enough to face whatever comes with courage and strength, but one is never old or wise enough to face some things. I am used to being many miles from you, so for me you have long been a lamp that burns bright in my mind day in and day out. I have been looking to that lamp these past few weeks and remembering many things, as I am sure you have too. I have recalled how rock-like you were when I was small. How we had to work together, you and I, to make the days run smoothly, how busy you were in the home…the view from the front room window, the Foresters cinema in Cambridge Heath, the cat Skinny and how pleased you were when you telephoned me at Aunt Ruby's and told me that you and Dad had just seen a wonderful flat that had a sliding door into the kitchen and we were going to live there. I have never known anybody with such a good sense of humor as you—you always had the knack of turning the most simple, insignificant event into something that we would laugh over until the tears rolled down our faces.

In families, especially, there are often endings that are not happy. And, having been through many, many happy endings, you and I have had to endure our own unhappy one. That may be the ultimate test of a relationship—to survive an unhappy ending like ours. But survive it we will. Because, in truth, there are no endings at all, no goodbyes. Those who are brought together for as many years as we have been can't be torn apart, and that has been my experience these last three years. The lamp that is you in my mind has burned just as brightly as ever.

I want to say Thank You to you for being my mother for seventy years. I think you know that I always loved you just a little more than I loved anyone else, and love never dies. It will stay with you throughout all time and overcome every obstacle, and when I think of you I will always see you smiling and laughing in your blue paisley dress that I loved so much. Don't be afraid, Mum, there are many hands reaching out to hold yours, not least of all mine. You're a good woman who has lived life with flair and intelligence and a strong heart. That will add up to a lot of brownie points!

You will always have my heartfelt love and gratitude for all that we've shared. God Bless you and keep you safe until we meet again,
Margaret

CHAPTER 11
My Hidden Family

January 1992. My brother, Tony, hugged me close, hardly able to suppress the sobs. He had only known of my existence for two weeks. My sisters had known for more than twenty years.

Tony had come to collect his daughters from Janie's house in the early evening. Janie met him at the gate with the girls. As he turned to leave she said, "You didn't know you had another sister, did you?"

What is it with this difficult-to-break news? He was stunned. Janie told him I was coming to meet them all in a few weeks. He went home in a state of shock and lay awake all night wondering where I was, what had happened and a million other things.

It was wonderful meeting my siblings—they talked about their childhood and told me their stories of remembered events. By the end of the weekend I was a much wiser woman. The siblings' stories were fun, Janie's were not so much fun. I had to slip back into old habits and sort the wheat from the chaff, knowing that I would probably never know the whole truth. I shrugged it off; after all, it was Janie's business and I had no way of proving whether it was true or false. I just had to accept what she wanted me to know. I'm still happy with that.

Chris, Janie's husband, was another thing altogether. There was the man who would have crushed me. Dark and handsome, like Frank, he had been a sailor, like Frank. Whereas Frank's war had been spent in Australia and China, Chris had been a regular and lived through the dangers of the North Atlantic crossings and the Allied landing at Salerno. He was truthful and loyal and had a mind that could fit into a capillary tube.

If I had been condemned to grow up with that man, with him not being my "real" father, I know I would have ended up on the scrap heap. If his heart ever turned against you it never turned back, and after a relatively short period of acquaintance he was complaining to Janie about me: I spent too long in the bathroom, the towels were out of place, I should be working in the kitchen, I behaved like a guest, etc., etc. He didn't bother to keep it quiet and I was always glad that my visits only lasted two or three days at a time.

To this day nobody in my hidden family has asked me how it was for me. They have all told me how it was for them.

Shortly after we had been reunited, Auntie Lucy, Janie's slightly younger sister, told the family that their father—my jolly Grandad Duns—had sexually abused her many times during her childhood.

He was a man that local people used to doff their hats to.

This triggered statements from the other sisters. All but one had suffered the same fate. The one who got away was on a different schedule to the others, which meant she had never been alone in the house with her father, lucky for her. That dreaded silence again had meant they could not seek support from one another and he was free to continue without hindrance. Well into her seventies, Janie would start to tremble when any mention of her father was made. The one who broke the silence, Lucy, did so as a result of counseling sessions. Janie had left home as soon as she could to live in the home of a school friend and her parents. She said it had been wonderful to feel safe and she had been happy in her new lodgings.

I didn't mention anything about my own experiences of abuse because I felt Janie might have felt some guilt about steering me toward it.

Whenever there was a family event I was there and we had a good time. Janie could put her finger on me in a way that Doll never could. She knew me from the inside out.

My lifestyle was a difficulty for them all, I think. I traveled a lot, did not call Janie every day (whereas I called Doll frequently), had no children and lived an independent life with the practice of meditation a large part of it.

Of Janie's three daughters, I was the only one who looked like her, and one of the most valuable things to me was a picture on Janie's mantelshelf of her own mother. It was like looking at me looking back. Janie's advances to Doll to attempt a reconciliation between the two had been met with stony silence, and after a while, Janie asked me how Doll was behaving toward me—had she adjusted to me finding my other family? I said she hadn't, not really. Janie's face screwed up, she wagged her finger at me and said, "Well, you did it, darlin'. You did it." I was certainly on my own with that one!

I am a holy man—a Dandi Swami—in the Vedic tradition of India. I am a very tall and thin man and I have a dandi stick, a bowl and a blanket as my only possessions. I am standing on the frozen edge of a huge icy wasteland. The wind is howling and it looks as though it should be difficult to stand. But I walk onto the ice, out beyond any shelter. I jam my stick into the ice and sit down, making a tent for myself out of the blanket. It goes over my head and covers my sides, overlapping in front of my face. As I settle I hear my own voice say, "It's all right, Mum. I'll just sit here and wait it out."

This is different from other visions: it does not seem to be about me as I am in this life or at another stage of life's development. Is it I who am the Dandi Swami? I certainly feel the ice beneath my feet and the razor harshness of the wind. He is silent and simply does what has to be done without flinching. His strength comes from within himself and is unsurpassed. This means he will outlive the frozen wastes around him and is not concerned about the discomfort he will have to endure. He is just the person I need to be to go through this.

When I hear my own voice address my mother, which mother is it? "Both" is the answer. In spite of all the trauma, the anger and resentment, they are both worried about the effects on me of this howling gale we are having to face. Although they cannot behave any other way than they are behaving on the surface level of life, on the inner level, the quantum level, there is compassion and the wish for all to be well. I make my statement in the vision in recognition of this fact and to reassure them that I will still be there at the end of it all.

I think that Janie thought I was going to be her daughter from now on and that Doll and Frank would take second place. That could never have happened, and over the years Janie realized that. She became very cool. They all became very cool. I was on the way to the perimeter again. During my visits, if family decisions had to be made they would all disappear into another room. I would hear those age-old whispers again and would try to read a book or newspaper. Then they would come back into the room as if nothing had happened. During the day I would discover what the decision had been by what transpired. The issue was always something concerning me but I had no voice. I was on the way to becoming an object again, but this time I was an adult in my late forties and could choose how to respond.

My youngest sister, Marie, saw that I was aware of what was going on behind the door and made some remark about it. I gently told her that if they wanted to do it that way it was their business, but perhaps they could inform me of their decision as though I were included and not wait for me to find out for myself.

It was all downhill after that.

They were my blood family, my kith and kin, but we were total strangers. Their experience of life was a million miles away from mine. How could we hope to bridge the gap?

Chris died in 2004. Janie had lost the love of her life. Marie lived closest to her and took the lion's share of the responsibility for her care, but she was very open about the fact that she felt Carrie, our other sister, and I should be prepared to drop everything to go and care for our mother. Janie's health had never been robust. Rheumatic fever as a child had left her with a heart condition, which culminated in major surgery when she was forty years old. Oddly enough, the surgery took place in the Royal London Hospital, which was only half a mile from where I was living with Doll and Frank. After that she had three-monthly checkups for the next thirty years. Three years after she and I had been reconciled, the doctors told her the condition was no longer considered life threatening and the checkups were not necessary.

But all those years of fragility took a toll on her body, which manifested itself after Chris's death.

At one point we were all gathered around Janie's hospital bed in the intensive care unit. She had been taken ill while visiting Carrie in Cornwall. A few beds away from her, and unknown to Janie, was a ten-month-old gypsy boy who had suffered an accidental head injury while in the care of his father.

The whole gypsy family was in the waiting room with us. The women were in one place and the men in another. The mother of the boy, Joe, wanted nothing to do with the father, who had steam coming out of his ears. We were in the middle.

On the second day I saw the doctor talking to the group of women. It was clear to me that the boy had just died and I covered my face and cried.

Riot police were called to the unit and arrived armed to the teeth. The mother had requested that the father not see the boy and the police were there to "keep the peace," wearing flak jackets and indestructible face shields and carrying rapid-fire rifles!

An hour or so later I was alone with Janie. I had had to walk past Joe's tiny body with all its tubes and his chubby little legs. Janie still had no idea of the drama being played out and we talked about this and that. Then Janie said how upsetting it was to hear a young girl crying her heart out at the bed at the end of the room. She said the young girl had stood there and broken her heart and Janie could hardly stand to hear her sorrow. I said something soft and held Janie's hand, all the while feeling chills down my spine for the mother at the end of the room saying goodbye to her child and the mother before me who had had to say goodbye to me as her child all those years ago. There we were, all together.

Janie recovered and returned to Surrey. She died in 2009 and the last time I saw her she was living in her own apartment in a retirement home and Marie was her primary caregiver. Janie and I spent quite a lot of time alone together during the three days I was there, but Janie seemed determined not to get into conversation. She had the television turned on the whole time, with the volume up high so we had to shout to hear one another even though we were less than three feet apart. I started crying as soon as I was out of the door when I left.

Marie had been very angry with Carrie and me after Chris's death because our lives had not been upset by the change, whereas she was now going back and forth to see our mother several times a week.

I had not addressed her comments as though I felt I had a duty to care for Janie. That seemed to fuel her anger and from then on she was stormy around me.

Did Janie's preoccupation with the television during my visit have anything to do with Marie's anger? I wonder. It would have been hard for Marie to hide it from Janie, and leaping assumptions play such a huge part in family dynamics.

But perhaps I had just been doing things wrong for all

those years and Janie simply did not want to bother with me. I'll probably never know.

Now that the anger was coming toward me from both families I felt the urge to survive in the best way I could. I maintained a friendly distance and clung to my own life like I was drowning.

Janie's death was like a dress rehearsal for Doll's. I was persona non grata. I had called from the US the day Janie died and repeatedly asked to be able to say goodbye to her, but it "wasn't convenient." I had booked my ticket to return to the UK, and because visa restrictions meant that I could not travel before the date on my ticket, I asked if the family could wait a day or two for my arrival to attend her funeral. To my continuing dismay, they held it two days before I got back.

They did, however, invite me to attend the disposal of Janie and Chris's ashes, which I did. The message was clear on that day: I was not welcome. They dumped me unceremoniously at the train station and sped off as fast as the Toyota could carry them.

Years have passed and slowly, slowly, we are making our way back to one another. My brother, Tony, has asked to hear from me and Marie has sent me some loving emails.

CHAPTER 12
A Harsh Truth

It is 1991. I am forty-six years old and with two friends who happen to be therapists. We have been working together on my spiraling struggle to stay sane since Janie decided not to see me. I am sitting in a chair next to a long dining table, deep in conversation.

Everything inside me goes dark. I am swirling around in some kind of dark matrix. It is not scary (I never feel fear during the visions) but I am filled with foreboding. Something is approaching and it is not good. It is an intention to harm. To harm me. I summon all my resources to look at this malevolence. I know myself to be helpless and I know this experience to be real. Something is coming for me and as it draws closer my mind works hard and fast to understand what it is. I am drawn deeper and deeper into the matrix and everything that this force is not melts away at its approach, until all that is left is what it is. It is the intention to murder.

I was seeing, as an adult, what had occurred during the first two months of my life—seeing that I had been a baby

*caught up in a demoniac web of Janie's desperation that saw
nothing but slammed doors all around. There was only one
alternative, only one solution. To do the deed. To murder.
Then the problem would be gone. I saw very clearly in an
instant that the force, that intention to stifle life, is a reality
more powerful than the desperation it uses as its tool.*

*I gradually come out of the swoon-like state I had slipped
into. It takes a while for me to be able to see out of my eyes.
Then all is clear and the colors of the room come back, then
the table, and there, at the end of the table, stands a figure
who is only half present in this world. It is a woman. She
is clothed in a dark blanket-like robe, but under the robe all
is light. I focus in on her face. She is smiling and I feel her
giving me love, giving me strength, giving me hope. She is,
and yet is not, Auntie Rose. Her face is the face of an Auntie
Rose who is without care, who is free. As I look at her I see
also myself.*

*The knowledge comes that this apparition is of a being who
is the essence of Auntie Rose, of me and of my heredity,
Auntie Rose's heredity. She stays just long enough for me
to understand and then melts away from sight. The terrible
knowledge that came to me as a memory in the matrix has
been robbed of its destructive power by the lady.*

*My birth mother had tried to murder me. She had put a
pillow over my face and squeezed her fingers over my nose.*

> *I had struggled. It was not as easy a thing to do as she thought. Her nerve had failed her. She removed the pillow. She would have to find another solution.*

There has never been any doubt in my mind of the veracity of this memory of the attempt by Janie to rid herself of her chains.

Years later, when Janie and I were alone together in her home, she looked across at me and said, "I didn't like you, you know. I didn't like you at all." I nodded dumbly. Our eyes met and locked together, and eternity entered us. We were one, and she longed to tell me what she had tried to do as I lay in my crib. She wanted to free herself of the terrible guilt. She told me in that silence and was spared having to speak out the words that would condemn her. It was a moment of the most powerful togetherness, terrible, terrible.

I had felt my heart stop beating the moment she gave utterance to her dislike of me. It seemed to take forever for it to summon the strength to carry on.

This is where I come face-to-face with another killer blow! Everything that happens from birth—and perhaps even before—is stored in the memory. A newborn baby is quantum in that it brings with it memories of the quantum reality that human society in general does not have access to. A newborn is not a "tabula rasa," a clean slate that has to be pressed into life and its rules. It brings with it the memory of the infinite. It is unbounded, all-knowing. It would not be possible to live in this world and retain all this knowledge, so we forget it quite early on. But it is still there, filed away in our deepest recesses.

As a newborn I would have felt Janie's distress, would have known what it was about. I would have been aware of what was going on around me and especially of any emotionally charged events.

This vision came before I met Janie. I knew the truth of it. I had to attempt to understand her desperation, her fear and shame.

It was so harsh and yet the consciousness of the baby was so clear and loving it protected me from any negativity and trauma. I had to know it because my demand was to know as much about myself as I could. This had been a major event and I feel that, by coming to me in this manner, it was robbed of its horror once and for all, but it had to be faced in order for that to happen.

The beautiful lady who seems to have been with me forever was there with me as part of the vision. Janie's dark secret could not live in her light, and I was rescued again.

I had known before I set out on my mission to find Janie that it may not go as I would hope—that there was no guarantee we would get on well with one another or even like one another. I had heard enough stories about these reunions to prepare myself as best I could for whatever came my way.

I heard her say many times that the most important thing in her life had always been her children. She had been an exemplary mother, it seemed, except for the mistake of having me. I had listened many times to her story of her as a young, single woman and the difficulties she had faced. Over time I accepted the fact that she felt she had done the right thing in parting with me—she had made the choice and gone for what she wanted most, a life with Chris—and she had no regrets. But she had guilt, of course, and sorrow.

I wouldn't say that I held myself back from her exactly, but I was always careful not to hope for too much from her. If she said something that broke my bones I would try to smile and nod encouragingly and give the impression that I understood. I felt that we owed one another nothing. At the back of my mind there lurked the knowledge that when the chips were down, when push came to shove and her back was against the wall, Janie had chosen to give me away. There was no sugaring of that fact possible once I returned to her.

We would look at one another in silence sometimes while the volumes of words disintegrated and we were left with only the surging tides of our own emotions. I knew the depths of her feelings were not to be touched by me. It was dynamite. And there was a bedrock of lack of trust from me that I never voiced but that stood like a sentry at my floodgates.

CHAPTER 13

Reflections

I am silent. Nothing stirs inside or outside. I find myself in a huge cavern of a place. I know it is cavern-like even though I cannot see a thing. It is so black my eyes do not have the range to adjust to its level. All my sense energy goes into listening, hearing. I feel an abandonment here, isolation, cold, and something very hard in the environment. Yet I know I am not alone. I feel the presence of others. I am standing upright and feel I want to move forward but realize that there may not be any ground beneath my feet if I move. I stay. There is a feeling permeating this place and now it approaches me. It is a feeling of nothingness: everything that comes to this place is nothing. No longer anything. Only my mind is able to function. I explore this place with my mind, this place of nothing. And yet it is not empty. It is full of something. As I open my mind to it, it allows me entry to this place at the edge of everything that is. I am at the very end of the line—the place where nothing and nobody wants to be. A word comes. Nonexistence. I am at the extreme of life. The negative extreme. I am standing in nonexistence. The recognition releases the environment to tell me more. I put out my hands and something is there. It is

rock. More than rock. It is the essence of rock—so hard even time has no dominion over it. There is still only blackness, but now my ears, that have been so alert for this time, are picking up some sounds. At first they are a blur on my own hearing mechanism, but they are changing, becoming more distinct. Now I hear a mumble and feel something move near me. The blackness and the rock forms itself into the shape of a living human and I can see it. Then there is more movement and other people emerge out of the rock. They join the sound, the mumble gets deeper, richer. These people, they are imprisoned, and I hear chains as they try to move but are held as on a leash by the rock.

Then the whole environment starts to move and I know I am surrounded by people fastened to the rock. The rock is all there is here. The mumble is no longer that. It is a cry that has been honed into something else. What is that something else? I strain my ears to perceive what I feel I hear. It has distinctness. It is not just a random sound of pain, of suffering. It is a song. All the sounds melt together into a rhythm, and structure emerges from this landscape inhabited by those who have been denied existence by the material world. The knowledge comes from within my own silence that slavery is here—of all nationalities, all genders, all times. Disability also. Disability of every kind— physical, mental, emotional. Everything unwanted is relegated to this place to become nothing. And yet they have preserved one thing—their ability to make sound. And they have created crooning, bleating, warm and hot songs. From the depths of my mind comes a vision of a concert hall with people in fancy clothes and flashing with jewelry, all sitting in rapt attention, listening to the songs of nonexistence. As each song finishes and the sound returns to the rock cavern, the concert hall explodes with its own sound. The audience is stamping its feet, standing and clapping and yelling. In recognition.

My visions do not come with explanations. In all cases I have found that they tell me the truth and give me knowledge—sometimes in advance and sometimes retrospectively—so that I can go through events in my life with confidence.

With this vision, however, I recognize that you, the reader, may be concerned by it because it seems quite "dark."

I imagine that the first assumption we may make is that this is a vision of hell. To be honest, I do not know through modern science or any other education system–based knowledge what this vision is about or where it comes from. However, I am extremely familiar with the process of conducting research into myself—using myself as the subject and object of my own experiment through the daily practice of meditation. This amounts to research into my own consciousness.

There is always knowledge, knowingness with every vision. It brings me knowledge through my own level of knowingness, and that level of knowingness is being constantly honed by the process of regular transcendence.

This vision, to me, is not about some life after death. It is about life in the here and now. It is about the inner life that we all have, and each of us has access to our own level of awareness of it.

The people relegated to the awful land of Nonexistence here in this vision are living people, and the vision is a vision of what actually takes place on an inner plane of the life of a human being.

To expand on my commentary above, I am suggesting here that when we experience denial of our identity as a full member of society with a full range of rights, respect and recognition, something happens to our inner life that cramps us, ties us down, restricts us, deprives us of the essence of our own lives, and perhaps this happens not on the physical plane of life but on a psychological, mental, emotional or social plane, all of which are planes belonging to the experience of life as a human being.

Even though inner, and therefore not apparent, these planes of experience are more powerful than we can imagine. Damage on any level of life will make its way to the surface and manifest itself as a form of negativity.

What quantum physics demonstrates to us is that damage to one person damages the whole world, because everything is connected to everything else.

It is in our interests to avoid damaging any other person, because what we do to others we do to ourselves—good and bad. That is the literal truth. We are always both the actor and the acted upon. Subject and object.

The concept of the scientist becoming the subject and object of their own experiment is not new to physicists. It is a concept born of quantum physics and automatically leads into a raging debate on the nature of consciousness.

A scientist believes that it is possible to know everything.

The quantum field questions us and asks us, "What do you mean by 'knowing'? Is your current definition of knowing adequate to enable you to understand what you want to know about the more subtle levels of the creation we call life?"

When we are interacting with such a powerful level of reality the demand is that the instrument with which we are knowing has to be as refined as what we are trying to know.

If we assume that the basis of all existence lies beyond the intellect, then perhaps there is some other faculty through which we can develop knowingness. Perhaps that faculty is our being itself. "Knowing by Being." The way to know about the subtle levels of life is to "be it." Hence the visions.

The intellect is, by its very nature, an instrument born of duality. It belongs to the complex levels of life where forces are separated out and choices have to be made—the level of everyday life as we know it, see it, feel it, touch it, hear it.

The field of quantum physics lies beyond duality. Its mechanics take place in subtler realms that are beyond our physical senses, realms where all forces are unified into wholeness. However, what we have is our intellect, so we use that intellect as it is in order to transcend the intellect itself.

The intellect is the vehicle that takes us to what it is we want to know, but it is not through the intellect that we know it. It is through our own being. Knowing by Being.

These subtle levels have to be experienced through our own human nervous system in order to be known.

This is why, I venture to suggest, the scientists need to turn within and conduct research on their own consciousness. This is not a new thought. Physicists are aware of this point of view. They are just trying everything else they can think of on the surface level of life to bring quantum to them before they turn to their own inner life and take themselves to quantum—just as in the 1920s the early quantum physicists did everything they could to cut quantum physics to fit the classical model before accepting that quantum has its own realities and needed a completely new approach.

This vision of the dark, rocklike place of nonexistence speaks directly to my feelings of non-belonging and the alienation of my own rights as a human being brought about by childhood experiences. However, terrible as the vision is, what comes out of it is not anger, the desire for revenge, madness. What comes out of it is a song. And not just any old song. A song that is deeply loved and appreciated by the audience, who celebrate it. Who recognize it. Because if one is alienated and sent to the land of Nonexistence it affects us all.

Given all the above, my birth mother, Janie, and I were in this together. Recrimination had no place in our relationship, but still it was not easy.

It would have been—and still would be—wrong of me to judge Janie in any way for her decision back then in 1945. That is the way it was in those days—I knew that only too well. But it meant that I knew where I stood with her for always. It had been one of those instances that take place on the razor edge of life—like on the field of combat—where you see beyond doubt which way a person falls when all is against them…when it's do or die. What matters most to them in that instant, their own survival or the survival of someone/something else? Such moments outlive the lives at stake. They are carried forever within the existence of those taking part. The outcome may be an indelible stain or a glorious light. It depends on the point of view held by the actors.

That is life. Life at the edge. We are always fortunate to experience it, to transform or be transformed by it.

I have a feeling there is much more to it, though. What if the one doing the giving away gives, at the same time, the responsibility for the act? It has to go somewhere. What if it goes to the one who is given away? Look around: they are not far away, those broken-down walking wounded with the lines and circles on their faces, with the "problems," the addictions, the dysfunction. Whose burden are they carrying? Their own? One of the most dangerous things in a society may be the jumping to conclusions, the assumptions made that display the level of ignorance it sets its codes by.

When we see a person going through their personal shipwreck, it is easy, first of all, to be glad we are not like them and also to assume that their own actions brought them to that place. "As you sow, so shall you reap" may in fact be the truth of their situation. But it is not for us to judge. The laws of nature that bring our destiny to us are unfathomable. It is more practical and more humane to see things as they are at the given moment—someone is being broken up by life's storms and tempests. They are a human being, like me, like you. That's all the information we need in order to give them a hand.

All of us know what it is like to be judged—and many of us will have had the sweet experience of not being judged. Being judged binds one, not being judged sets one free. Why would a mother want to give away her own child? Because of society's judgment, which is unbearable. Once the child has gone elsewhere the mother may feel some relief for a while, but then the memory, the heart, the guilt kick in. Over years it is enough to drive a woman insane. On the surface she may be perfectly happy, may find someone to share her life with and bring up children. On the inside, however, she has to work at burying the torment deeper and deeper to keep the truth away. Losing a child, no matter what the circumstances, is a life-changing experience.

For the child there is a different kind of torment: the feeling of being discarded, of being without a mother even if you find a new one, whether you "know" your own origins or not. New parents may be perfect in many ways, but in many cases the child feels they are somewhere they do not belong, even though they may be well loved. Which translates into feeling they do not belong anywhere. This desolation can get them into trouble, and once in trouble it is difficult to get out. A reputation may grow of being unreliable, unstable, unsociable.

They were born a problem. Their very existence caused their mother anxiety. They are issue and they carry the mother's and father's issues with them throughout their life. They carry the burden and have to do with it what they can.

Of course, of course, it's not always like that, says society in its attempts to avoid responsibility. I'm sure that is absolutely true. I myself have never come across one of the perfect ones, but there's always tomorrow.

Most of a human being is "under the wire." What we see in our daily interactions with others are tips of icebergs. Most of what makes us real happens out of sight, buried in hearts and memories. It is the same for all of us. If you manage to live your life without coming up against forces that defeat you now and again you are very unlucky. If we are defeated and know it and glimpse what is there in our own depths as a result, we can count ourselves fortunate. It's not bad down there. Some of the best people come from there. They may have had to suffer the loss of their loved ones, their home, their country, their reputation: they may be relegated to the edges of normality, but they have seen what goes on under the wire. They are the future.

I am lying on my stomach at the edge of a huge, dry quarry, peering over the edge. On the floor of the quarry in clear sight is a ramshackle shed made of corrugated iron. I see a figure beside one of the exposed walls of the shed. It is a man in an overcoat and he flattens himself against the thin wall as he becomes aware of a gang of young men coming toward the shed from behind.

In front of the shed on the ground is a scrappy piece of corrugated iron about five feet square. I know this to be significant to the man in the overcoat. Strangely enough I see only that when the group of men comes around to the front of the shed, the man emerges from the shadows. I do not see what happens between them, only that the whole group runs away back in the direction from where they came. The lone man is standing near the piece of iron and I see very clearly that he is Rod Steiger.

Then I am on a hillside near the quarry. It is sandy. I am buried up to my neck in the sand. I cannot move except to turn my head. When I do this I see a foot close to my right ear. It is wearing a rough sandal like those worn by ancient Roman soldiers. The soldier passes very close to my head and is walking slowly to the top of the hill. When I strain to move my head I see a plumed helmet and the hardened face of a seasoned warrior. He seems unaware of my presence, but now I know what he is thinking. He climbs to the top of this hill every day. It is one of his duties. There is nothing going on so there is never any need to hurry. When he gets to the top he looks out over the foreign landscape to line after line of hills. His sharp eyes are looking for signs, but he sees none.

After a while he sighs deeply, wondering how much longer he has to stay in this unyielding place that never tests his mettle, never brings him any interest. There is no question, however, of him leaving. It is his duty to stay and do what he does and he is bound, body and soul, by his duty.

Now the scene changes again. I am at the bottom of the quarry, near the shed, and the ancient warrior is with me. We are silent. He has fashioned a chair out of a long, long piece of rope—so long I cannot see the end—and he moves the piece of corrugated iron away to reveal a big hole in the ground. I am now in the chair and the warrior is lowering me into the hole, releasing the rope little by little so that I remain stable and move smoothly. I can easily touch the sides of the hole. It becomes darker and darker and I feel the rough sides and can smell the earth. It is completely silent and the warrior lowers me deeper and deeper, so that I am lost to the surface and am only aware of the walls surrounding me. They are changing as I go deeper. The smell of the earth is more fragrant, like the smell of coal. My nose is almost touching the wall and my fingers move on the surface, feeling stones and edges. But there is something almost gentle here. I feel welcome, as though I belong, as though I am going to be told something valuable.

Deeper and deeper I go, always aware that I owe my safety to the warrior on the surface. It is completely black. Is there a bottom? I do not know. But there is something... something...I take a huge breath and let the chasm in. Yes! Yes! I know what is here but I will have to go even deeper to reach it. Gold is here. Gold.

The warrior and Rod Steiger were one person.

Steiger was the hero of the social scene—warding off all intruders, maintaining precious solitude in that vast, unfriendly space.

The warrior was the hero of the solitude. He did not enjoy his posting but endured it because he was duty personified. Where his orders came from I do not know. Was the fact that I was buried up to my neck in the sand a device to tell me that I was like the dust at his feet? That would seem appropriate.

I felt they were both there specifically for my sake. Why that should be remains a mystery.

As with every vision, this one is as fresh as the moment I became aware of it, and throughout it I felt nothing but safety, love and caring around me. There never is any room for fear.

What did I get from it, then? I'm still trying to work that out, but as I write my story here, I find myself thinking about life "under the wire"—the metaphor for which is my being lowered into the hole in the ground. Thinking about the life of all of us. The lives of those who are literally forced under the wire by conflict, war, illegal acts, undesirable race, religion, etc.

Perhaps we will discover very soon that, whether it's running a country or just one life, a particularly valuable wisdom resides with those who are familiar with life "under the wire," "on the edge," "not quite up to the mark"—those we "would not invite to dinner." They may be able to tell us a lot about the consequences of those decisions made in moments of truth, because that's where they live. It's where they come from, that region of humanity that is out of sight and which determines the path of our lives. They've never left it. They carry it always. It's a new definition for heroics.

"Under the wire" may be high class, with a lot of money, a fantastic career, a "normal" lifestyle. We all deal with it in our own way and some get rounds of applause, standing ovations. Others wait at borders, walk seven miles for water each day, see their children starve, hide from falling bombs, sell drugs, live on the streets, get drunk every night, watch TV every night, pray none of it ever happens to them…

What if the one doing the giving away of a child is actually making the supreme sacrifice? What if they are doing what has to be done in order for that human being to develop as they have to? What if the away-giver turns out to be the hero—bearing a lifetime of the most awful guilt for an act that really was for the best? There's a thought. What will we do with that thought? Does it all come down to our point of view? Which version of the act of giving away will we go for? Do we choose our own belief system in life and then have to live it out? Where is the nugget of gold in a human life?

The ones who live below the wire will be first to find the gold. The future belongs to them, because having to mine your own resources can make you wise, can make you strong, can make you unafraid, can help you to carve a future out of solid rock.

What we have to remember always is that there is more than one possible future lying ahead of us. How we respond to the story of the lost child will determine our future. How the child responds to their own story will determine her or his future. Will they and we choose a response that expands our horizons or shrinks them? And is it possible to know before we respond what the result of that response will be? That question must hang in the air for a while longer.

CHAPTER 14
Connecting the Dots

The possibilities are endless in a quantum world. Such a huge statement about the effects of human response demands a little background information, and I hope not to lose your interest if I attempt to provide a little of that.

The view of endless possibilities existing together in a quantum world is now part of our understanding of quantum physics. But it was not always that way. In his book *Quantum*, Manjit Kumar tells how the two greatest scientists in the world, Albert Einstein and Niels Bohr, did battle in the early days over the very nature of this new model of reality. Both men knew that quantum is correct, but each was driven to their limits by the desire to prove their own point of view by experiment. Bohr succeeded well but was haunted by Einstein's insistence that reality had an existence independent of observation.

Bohr's so-called "Copenhagen Interpretation," developed by his team of physicists in Denmark's capital city, declared that there was no objective reality, that reality only appeared when it was observed. Einstein, however, forever grappled with his intuition that quantum mechanics was not complete in itself—that it was, in fact, part of a greater system, which Einstein called his "unified field theory."

Both men died with these differences in philosophical standpoint unresolved and nagging, nagging in the brain of physics. Bohr's position was predominant at that time and remained so for many years, while Einstein was relegated to the wilderness as an old scientist who could not see past his own relativity.

In July 1957 a PhD thesis was published at Princeton University written by the twenty-six-year-old physicist Hugh Everett III, titled On the Foundations of Quantum Mechanics. This thesis revived Einstein's view, as Everett demonstrated that all possibilities are present in every experiment, where every quantum possibility coexists as an actual reality in an array of parallel universes: the "many-worlds interpretation." This meant that the vilification of Einstein had to be seriously reconsidered: the revered Copenhagen interpretation had been found wanting. Everett's thesis and the discoveries of the weak and strong nuclear forces led to the search for a unified field theory becoming the "holy grail" of modern physics.

As I write this, I am aware from a physicist friend—a dinner table revelation if you like—that a recent hypothesis states that, in fact, what is observed by the subject is not actually changed by the attention of that subject. It is merely perceived by the observer to have changed. This means that any change that has taken place has done so within the consciousness of the subject only while the object of attention remains, in fact, unchanged. This would challenge the Copenhagen Interpretation referred to earlier. It may herald the beginning of the physicist turning within.

The stage nowadays is occupied by theoretical physicists who know that they will never be able to construct an experiment with equipment big and powerful enough to prove their new and science-fiction-sounding points of view. We have taken the whole mission beyond the physical and classical range.

Time to take another direction, to go inside the observer. Time, in fact, to go "under the wire," where we may well find that quantum mechanics, the nuts and bolts of the quantum physics umbrella, resides—and plays—within the unified field of all the laws of nature, the unified field where all the forces come together and exist in unmanifest, pure potential. Where the parallel universes are born.

The only way to test that theory is for the observer scientist to conduct research into their own consciousness. They may well find themselves concluding, as I do, that it is difficult to determine a right action from a wrong one when there are only ever events based on human points of view, human choices, human consciousness. It is not the quarks, leptons, photons, electrons, etc. that are the reality. It is we humans. We are the final reality.

This knowledge helps. It helps me, as a baby out of the blue, come to terms with the decisions made by others that laid out the blueprint for my life without my permission. There are so many possible points of view that moral judgment becomes irrelevant.

And this may be so even in the case of my own experience of sexual abuse.

I have to come to terms, also, with the concept of responsibility. Things that occurred when others were responsible for my welfare have to be allowed to dissolve into insignificance. They are no longer relevant. What is relevant is my own future and for that I, alone, am responsible. I have to acquire a set of responses to my life that enables me to look forward without the tinge of rancour spreading like a stain. The Oxford English Dictionary defines the word "responsibility" as "the ability to respond." That is what I now focus on: my ability to respond to events from a space within myself that is clear, clean and based on a world view that comes from my experience of life, and not the experience of those whose influence on me is outdated. It makes living a much more exciting and "now" experience.

Far from causing more confusion, this opens the door to my freedom. It all depends on me, how I choose to see it. I can test that out and see how it feels to be judgmental or non-judgmental, closed and prohibiting or open and accepting. How does it make me feel to be any of these, and which will I settle on? Whichever it is, that is the reality I will have made for myself and I will have to step into it and live it out. Because it is all about me. Nothing but me. When my consciousness abides at the quantum level I am the subject, object and process of observation of my own experience. That dynamic of *three-in-one* creates me as the verifier. The reality of quantum physics becomes verified by my being quantum physics itself for as long as my consciousness rests at that level of life.

It therefore follows that it is also all about you. Nothing but you. You and me. Alone and together in this fantastic playground of quantum multiverses.

I believe my visions demonstrate that what we know as "everyday life" is just one aspect of reality, that there are multiple realities available to us. The choice of reality is ours, and on that choice depends everything that follows.

There is a reality where trauma/stress has no place and there exists only the joy of living a fulfilled and constructive life based on a level of knowledge we have not yet fathomed. I have had glimpses of that reality, and just a few glimpses were enough to carry me through a life here on earth that could have had a dangerously negative effect on my future. I want to identify with that blissful, joyful reality and hold the view that the way to achieve that is to become more simple, more subtle, even childlike, and in the process to develop the wisdom to be all those things without sacrificing knowledge and experience of this wonderful world.

Wherever my visions come from, they show me that I don't have to die in order to experience a higher level of life.

I so much want to understand it all—to do it justice—and I'm such a beginner, a circle, always ending at my beginning, always leaving and returning home.

I am going to leave my story here, with you. Whatever you think of it, it will continue and continue to be a search for truth—the kind of truth that never changes and that can send us reeling, because it is not dependent on our acceptance for its validity. Like a soft, leathery bloodhound I will search and search for more interpretations and keep testing them out. That is the greatest experiment of all.

I wish you good luck with your own journey back to yourself, back to your home—whichever path you choose.

Conclusion

I have experienced a tremendous amount of love in my life. Doll and Frank loved me in their own way, and Doll and I had many, many good times over the years. Whatever stresses we encountered on the way to one another played havoc with us. In spite of all the rage and inner conflict, we suffered together what the years brought us, and together we rejected one another. It has been a togetherness of a different kind—an unwanted togetherness—and it created a bond of its own. My love for Doll has always been invincible and I am still learning to love Frank. As time went by I came to see Doll's vulnerability more and more clearly. She never lost her lust for power or her love of seeing those close to her wither under her razor-sharp wit. But there were occasions when I saw the mask fall away to reveal a crumpled person gasping for her life. At those times I would place myself between her and any perceived threat and would have been happy to die defending her. She was my true mother and her extraordinariness pushed me out of the nest to find my heart's desire. If she had been the kind of mother who stayed at home and baked and hummed sweet songs I would have happily stagnated by her side.

The legacy of shared repulsion lives on between some of those who are closest to me. But the rest of the world and me... there is nothing but love there. I have friends in abundance and many of them know me better, have lived with me longer, than my close family. It is the same with my extended family.

A wise pundit once told me that I could live with anyone I chose and be very happy with them, but I should never marry because as soon as I marry I become a victim. I would add to the pundit's wisdom that as soon as my relationship with someone becomes legally binding, by adoption as well as marriage, it starts to fall apart!

I had already been married three times when given that sage advice. When my inner eye glances over the third marriage I find myself thinking "I won't go there!" Some things are best just forgotten. (It was awful, dear reader, awful.) However, now that I have received that "victim" perspective from someone who, like me, is familiar with forces of life that remain hidden, I know to remain single for the rest of my time.

The single me is much more content, and I would say more creative, than the married me. When I spoke to a different pundit at a different time about my seeming to have the mentality of a scapegoat, he looked at me for a long time before telling me that is "to do with the circumstances of [my] birth."

Victim. Scapegoat. Neither of those descriptions sits well with my outgoing personality, which may be why I have faced so many storms when I have stood up against these negative determinations of my nature. I have decided that "victim" and "scapegoat" are going to have to go. I have the strong desire to set out my own brand-new template of what is me. It is going to be a template that brings positive feedback in abundance. Perhaps I am going to have to learn to live permanently "under the wire," without the proper paperwork, just like the babies who come out of the blue.

I find the thought of that liberating. I never have been

able to complete even the most simple official form without throwing a fit. To be unofficial is to be the eagle, the summit of the world, the blank white page, the hidden—to return to my source and know it for the first time. Will I begin again? First I think I will devote my time to studying life's natural laws to see if I can come up with a better deal! My "something" will help me with that. And the transcendence will light my way.

My something—whatever it is that takes me to the quantum level of life—is bliss. Simply bliss. Somehow I have retained a link with it throughout my life, even though it feels independent of me and yet I am a part of it. I am not able to say that it is me or that I am it. It feels greater than me and yet it gives me all of itself now and again. It is intelligent. At times when I have felt dispossessed and without choices, it has made me feel a profound sense of belonging to everything in the universe and has opened the way to multiple choices.

Is my something God, then?

I can understand the need to put my something in a box, to give it a label so that it can rest in its proper place on the mental shelf. But I feel I have to disappoint anyone with this ambition.

Nothing in my visions has ever said to me "This is God speaking" or given any definite indication that would identify the experience as godly or holy. And yet I think about it a lot. It would be very nice to have a direct relationship with the Almighty and know it to be that. Very comforting. I am always left with the same thought: every living being has their own relationship with the divine already. What's surprising about that?

In the case of my visions, if I have to put them in some kind of language that will categorize them, make them easier to understand, I would say it may be that they provide me with evidence of the existence of a supreme intelligence. They come to me time and time again and the content is always unique, while certain important aspects of them remain always the same. They are always blissful, during and after the experience, they always bring me comfort, peace, joy, and they always, always, uplift me and dispel my fears. And it always feels like the same "thing" coming again and again—the content is always different but the medium feels the same, always the same.

Perhaps God doesn't come and shake us by the hand. Perhaps S/He sends evidence and waits for us to notice. I cannot say, because I do not consider myself an authority on God. I just know that my "something" has saved my life many times, that it is loving and intelligent and creative and very powerful. If it were ever to identify itself to me in words, I would be thrilled and very surprised! I do not expect that to happen. And I just love the evidence, which touches me with the lightness of a feather and yet changes my life completely. As with the vision of my father:

When I had the vision of opening my arms to my father I knew very clearly that something good had happened to our relationship. Living through the next twenty years with him, I was able to respond creatively to impulses in the environment and thus make the best out of a particular state of affairs, because I knew what had happened. And the knowing was on such a level that no new trauma was created. Even though my gut reactions to Frank remained the same, I possessed information that allowed me to see signals of something different on the horizon. Our relationship began to expand where it had been contracting for so long. I see that as nothing short of a miracle.

But all that is still not reason enough to write it down. It is all material that I have kept very private, some of it for almost seventy years now, and there would have to be a magnificent reason for wanting to write about it after all this time.

The magnificent reason is the future. It is quantum. The present and the past, too, are quantum. Now that quantum physics has been around for a hundred years or so, we are beginning to realize that there really is much more to life than we thought. And it comes right down to the individual.

My "something" is quantum. The visions are real. They carry information and the energy to transform. They carry me into a future that I want and I become a full participant in my own life. They give me the feeling of having more control.

People have always had these visionary experiences. They are as old as humanity. We have always put them in a box labeled "The Unknown"—and sometimes we have put the individuals in a box also.

With quantum physics we are becoming familiar with a new level of the unknown. We may not ever fully know it, but we can explore it and make friends with it and reap the many benefits it can bestow. A new frontier. The way to it lies through our own experience. In fact, it has to be experienced to become enlivened.

My own life was so extreme when it came to the field of my own being that I had to delve deeply into my reality to verify my existence. I believe that delving took me to subtler levels of consciousness that allowed me to come upon a place where the hidden was revealed and I could feel at home.

This finding was such an effective tool, the at-home feeling so strong, that it overcame everything everyday life could throw at it.

Transcendence was the key that unlocked the mystery for me.

Regular practice of the Transcendental Meditation technique from the age of thirty-two gave me access to the space within myself where my "something" takes residence. As a result, the relationship between us became two-way. I could go to it, as well as it coming to me.

For all of us, the future is quantum. And the road to it lies through the development of our own consciousness. The outcomes of circumstances in our lives are not set in stone. If we have access to the appropriate level of consciousness there are ways in which we can determine outcomes for ourselves. We can change what happens.

This book has been a tale of exploration into a life that had been bound by restriction and untruth and, by becoming its own research study into consciousness and diligently treading a path of balance—by becoming its own living fulcrum—has found its own truth and eternal nature within its own prison walls.

The chances of my becoming a prisoner of the state were pretty high with my background. An authoritative article I once read said that 80 percent of the British prison population was made up of people who had been separated from their mother while very young. Yet I did not go to prison. I didn't become addicted to alcohol or drugs and I didn't decide that I liked animals better than humans. Mine was the mentality that just "carried on." I staggered through my life, learning not to do some things twice, taking delight in things I did that worked well.

Which all means that I was extraordinarily lucky. Not wise, not good. Just lucky. Lucky not to have become pregnant outside or inside marriage. Inside marriage it would have changed all priorities and I would have happily and willingly given my future to my offspring. But then, I might have learned some powerful lessons at their expense. Not a good way to learn. Better not to have a blessing in the first place than to have it and waste something beautiful. Outside marriage I might have had to face the same concerns as Janie or Doll—and then what would I have done? I shudder to think.

But children there have been, and many of them. Some I have lived with for many years and others I have set eyes on for just a few moments. Their story belongs elsewhere, but they stretch themselves across time and space and tap my shoulder with the reality of their existence. It is a case of recognition of something that belongs—I to them and they to me. They are my own babies out of the blue. We share our existence, these children and I, knowing that separation is not only not possible but also not desired by any of us. We appear to one another sometimes, like bit-part actors in a play. We speak our lines and smile our smiles and then exit stage left. The party is set to begin backstage when the curtain finally falls.

Perhaps I will write all that out one day.

What I have written here is the story of just one life among millions who have experienced the same things as I. It is a tale of separation, of a huge rift in relationships, of giving up, giving in, giving out, starting and restarting. There are people here whom I will probably never see or speak to again because we have broken down along the road. And yet we belong to one another. They belong to me and I belong to them. That is one thing about us all that will never change, despite all the fights, accusations and recriminations. Belonging is natural to life. It doesn't end just because we all fall out with one another. Falling out just brings the illusion of separation, but there's no way we can be separated from one another. Race, gender, color, creed, species even, are of no significance when it comes to belonging.

We belong each to the other whether we like it or not.

We are quantum.

The Vedic texts contained in the Vedic literature, the oldest written body of knowledge in the world, written by rishis— seers of reality out of their own direct experience of the source of life—tell us that truth is "that which never changes." So, what if scientists discover some other great system, some other reality: will that render what is said in this book untrue? Does quantum physics have a shelf life? It may well be the case that it does. But the human experience of the visions never changes. They represent truth. Whatever else may be discovered will be what has been outlined here but perhaps under another name. All that may have to happen is for our understanding to reach new levels.

This book presents us with the knowledge that truth can come to us, so while we strive and strain to make our way toward it, we may well find that it meets us halfway. We are all doing our very best to make the introductions as smooth as possible.

Satyam Eva Jayate
Truth Alone Triumphs
Mundaka Upanishad 3.1.6

Afterword

Through all this experiencing, learning, falling down and relearning, the support of Auntie Rose has been there, quiet and loving and good-humored.

My life has been scattered with precious gems when it comes to people, and Auntie Rose stands out as my jewel in the crown. It's not that I saw much of her, because I have hardly seen her at all, but her presence has been a symbol of my identity, my authenticity as a person. She has been steadfast throughout all the madness that overtook me and has always thought about my welfare, how it must have been for me. In fact, I think she has thought about it much more than I ever have. Whatever I could do for her would not be enough to demonstrate how much I love her and how grateful I am to her for her love of me and clearsighted understanding that someone in my situation cannot take life for granted—we have to search for our path through life and often find ourselves lost in the undergrowth in the process!

Auntie Rose has been my fulcrum until I was integrated enough to take that role for myself. She has been courageous and supportive on my behalf and may well be one of the main reasons why, when I think of this life that I carry around with me, I consider myself one of the luckiest people on earth.

APPENDIX I

Qualities of My "Something"

My "something" is indescribable, and the only way I can think to convey to others what it is, is to set out qualities that are always present when I experience it. Here are forty-six aspects of it that I have come to think of as evidence of the existence of a higher intelligence that relates itself to me:

1. It comes very gently
2. It communicates
3. It informs
4. It relates itself to me
5. It is always a surprise
6. It brings guidance
7. It is always concerned with me and the course of my life
8. It unifies
9. It transforms
10. It loves me unconditionally
11. It is always present
12. It is all-knowing
13. It protects
14. It is wise
15. It is beyond time and space
16. It is nurturing
17. It is the essence of bliss
18. It is all-powerful
19. It is humility

20. It is accepting
21. It is liberating
22. It is intelligent
23. It is the essence of giving
24. It is compassionate
25. It is non-judgmental
26. It is authenticity
27. It is natural
28. It is reassuring
29. It is truth
30. It is compelling
31. It is nonintrusive
32. It is leadership
33. It is service
34. It is always with me
35. It is trustworthiness
36. It is freedom
37. It is whole
38. It is full
39. It has ownership
40. It demonstrates
41. It has energy
42. It is universal
43. It adopts individuality to itself
44. It is undemanding
45. It is always new
46. It knows no limits

APPENDIX II

Effects of My "Something"

Here are twenty-seven ways in which my "something" affects me every time I experience it:

1. It is pacifying
2. It brings me unconditional love
3. It brings me knowledge: of itself; of me
4. It dispels fear
5. It inspires
6. It expands my awareness
7. It guides my thoughts
8. It has the ability to transform outcomes in my life
9. It brings me comfort
10. It brings me companionship
11. It knows me (better than I know myself)
12. It brings me a sense of belonging
13. I feel cherished by it
14. It brings me strength
15. The memory of it remains clear and sharp throughout time
16. It allows me to be active beyond time and space
17. It allows me to experience freedom that lasts
18. It brings me bliss
19. It makes me happy in my life regardless of circumstances
20. It is my friend

21. It is at my service
22. It is a gift to me
23. It brings me a truth I long for
24. It reassures me
25. It never leaves me; I leave it
26. It gives me all of itself without depleting itself
27. It is an "everything" that becomes individual for my sake

Bibliography and Suggested Reading

Material Relating to Ancient Vedic Science

Claes, Joachim. The Field Paradigm: 20 Experiments that Can Change the World. Joachim Claes, 2017.

Mahesh Yogi, Maharishi. Celebrating Perfection in Education. Fairfield, IA: Maharishi University of Management Press, 1997.

Inaugurating Maharishi Vedic University. Fairfield, IA: Maharishi University of Management Press, 1996.

Maharishi Mahesh Yogi on the Bhagavad-Gita. London: Penguin, 1969.

Nader, Tony. Consciousness Is Primary: Illuminating the leading Edge of Knowledge. Fairfield, IA: Maharishi University of Management Press, 2013.

Material Relating to Modern Science

Al-Khalili, Jim. *Quantum: A Guide for the Perplexed*. New York and London: Weidenfeld & Nicolson, 2003.

Davies, Paul. *God and the New Physics*. New York: Simon & Schuster, 1983.

Gribbin, John. *In Search of Schrödinger's Cat: Quantum Physics and Reality*. New York: Bantam Books, 1984.

Kaku, Michio. *Hyperspace: A Scientific Odyssey Through Parallel Universes, Time Warps, and the 10th Dimension*. New York: Oxford University Press, 1994.

Kumar, Manjit. *Quantum: Einstein, Bohr, and the Great Debate About the Nature of Reality*. New York: Norton, 2008.

Material Relating to Transcendental Meditation

Rosenthal, Norman E. *Super Mind: How to Boost Performance and Live a Richer and Happier Life Through Transcendental Meditation*. New York: Tarcher Perigee, 2016.

Roth, Bob. *Strength in Stillness: The Power of Transcendental Meditation*. New York: Simon & Schuster, 2018.

Related Articles

"Quantum Physics Came from the Vedas: Schrödinger, Einstein and Tesla Were All Vedantists" (blog), at http://www.krishnapath.org/quantum-physics-came-from-the-vedas-schrodinger-einstein-and-tesla-were-all-vedantists/

"Dalai Lama: Spirituality without Quantum Physics Is an Incomplete Picture of Reality" by Kalee Brown, at http://www.collective-evolution.com/2017/04/26/dalai-lama-spirituality-without-quantum-physics-is-an-incomplete-picture-of-reality/

About the Author

Margaret Rose Duns lives a peaceful yet thoroughly exhilarating life as part of a community of women committed to creating the criteria necessary to bring permanent peace on earth through the effects of the daily practice of meditation. As the years pass, the commitment grows stronger, and with that come new directions, new activities—like writing—and a greater reverence for life.

She is currently living in New York.